MY FRIEND PAUL

MY FRIEND PAUL

**A Novel
By Alfred H. Yale**

Library of Congress Cataloging in Publication Data

Yale, Alfred H.
  My Friend Paul.

  1. Paul, the Apostle, Saint—Fiction. 2. Luke, Saint—Fiction. I. Title.
PS3547.A36M9   1986   813'.54   85-27299
ISBN 0-8309-0433-6

Printed in the United States of America

DEDICATION

This book is dedicated to those eager for the knowledge, truth, and love that Christ can bring into their lives.

INTRODUCTION

The writing of this book was completed before our father's death in 1984. We, his daughters, have submitted this our father's last manuscript, for publication as a special tribute to him and his love for the life and works of Paul.

Who is Paul? What does he have to do with us today?

Paul was a prominent citizen who led a very colorful life. In his earlier years he was not a Christian, but he knew what he believed. If something was wrong he acted to correct it. No one pushed him around. Only God was able to change the course of his life.

The scriptural account of Paul captured the attention of our father, and he decided to learn all he could about this unusual man. The more he learned, the more he felt he knew Paul, and he wanted to share this knowledge with others. It was so important to him that he wrote a textbook, *The Life and Letters of Paul.* He found that this was not enough, however. The story needed to be told in yet another way. He wanted to capture Paul's spirit in a novel and introduce him to others as the friend he had come to know.

After our father retired in 1974 he was able to find time to make this dream a reality. As the story formed in his mind, he began to write it. With the onset of terminal illness he pushed ahead, anxious to finish the book. He wanted to refine areas in it but his health failed before he was able to do so. Thus the manuscript remains as originally written.

The life of our father can be compared to the life of Paul. Both were active and studied to learn God's ways as they matured in years. As they learned they grew, accomplishing their goals and standing by their beliefs. Being reared a Methodist, our father studied and learned all he could about that doctrine and later became a minister for the church, thus accomplishing one of his goals. Both men were content in their beliefs, but God wanted more from them and turned their lives around. Paul met God on the way to Damascus and was shown how to reach out and bring more than just Jewish people to the faith. Into our father's life God brought a "Mormon" wife (our mother, Miriam Winholtz). Even though he tried to prove the doctrines of her church wrong, God showed him the answers to his questions. This led him to the point where he was ready to change his life and join the Reorganized Church of Jesus Christ of Latter Day Saints. Both Paul and our father accepted God's challenge and went forth in active service. They dedicated their whole beings to doing what God expected of them.

Paul, an educated man, went on to learn even more. He discovered God's ways and used his knowledge to help others. Our father was also educated, and as he continued his studies he gained new understanding of God's teachings. This made him better able to help others. He studied the Greek language because he realized that various versions of the Bible contained different meanings due to the translater's interpretations. He wanted to be able to read the scriptures as they were originally written before any translation was made. This knowledge he passed on to all he met, and his understanding of Greek became a tool of great value in teaching God's Word.

Our father wanted to share his love and respect for Paul. He wrote this book for no one person but for all who desired to meet his friend.

As God worked in the lives of the apostles of old, so he

continues to work in people's lives today. We present this book so others can share a view of Paul and enjoy him as a "friend." We also challenge each reader to

know your God;
know what he expects of you;
step out in faith and be active;
serve God all the days of your life.

Eleanor Marie Yale Lewis, Littleton, Colorado
Nancy Louise Yale Kwak, Madison, Wisconsin
Maxine Miriam Yale Bailey, Tenino, Washington

Chapter 1

I was awakened by a pounding that seemed to surround me as I struggled up out of a sound sleep. It continued as I swung my feet over the side of my bed and felt for the floor. Mumbling some uncomplimentary remarks about those who would interrupt a man's sleep I called, "Patience! Patience! I hear you!"

Cautiously I peered from my window. In the darkness I saw shadowy figures before my door.

It had been scarcely a week since the robbers had pounded on this same door. One of their number, they said, had been wounded. When I had let them in, the leader brandished his sword and thrust it against my chest. "Fix his wound," he demanded. "If he dies, you die." And the man continued to stand menacingly before me.

Pushing his sword aside with more calm than I felt inside, I moved to the wounded man's side. Blood seeped through the crude bandage they had tied about him. When I removed the bandage I found that he had been slashed across the abdomen, and his innards were pushing through the gaping wound. Turning to my table I began to thread a needle.

"It will take strong men to hold him while I close the wound," I said.

The leader motioned to two of his followers. They grabbed the wounded man to immobilize him, and I set about the task of sewing his flesh together.

Even as I worked, there was a shout from outside the house. Soldiers were coming. The leader stood threateningly, as if it were my fault that they were being attacked. "Say not a word if they come in," he ordered, and then faded back into the shadows of the stairway.

Hardly had he done this than the door burst open, and soldiers poured into the room. Next came their captain. He took in the scene and indicated by a nod that I was to continue. Not a word was spoken, but the men spread out and quickly discovered the leader and dragged him into the light. They started to pull the two men who were helping me and I spoke. "Do not do that!" I commanded. "This patient must remain immobile."

The captain spoke to two soldiers. They stepped forward and, as the two malefactors were placed under arrest, the soldiers took their places.

I completed the sewing and bandaged the wound. Sweat dripped from my chin. It was a very tense moment, for I knew that I might be charged with aiding the criminals.

"Do you know who these men are?" asked the captain.

"No."

"Have you ever seen them before?"

"No!"

"Why did they come to you for aid?"

"Perhaps because I am well known as a physician in this city."

"Yes, I know of you," the captain said. He went on, "These thieves have moved into the city from out of the mountains. We have made it unprofitable for them along the highway, so they have begun to prey on the merchants and citizens who might be out at night. They tried.to rob the inn, but the keeper and his friends routed them. This man," he turned and pointed to my patient, "was wounded in the fight."

"But why would they take chances of being caught by coming to me?" I asked.

"This is the brother of their leader."

"What will happen to them?"

"That is up to the court of Caesar," was the reply. "But I venture that they will die. They have killed many in their depredations."

With this, he turned to leave. "It is well that you have a good reputation in this city, Luke, or I might have charged you with abetting these men."

— — —

Scenes of this recent event flooded my memory as I tried to identify those who were at my door. I could make out only two figures. One seemed to be holding the other erect.

"What do you want?" I called.

"Is this the home of Luke the physician?" the taller man called, raising his voice to make himself heard.

"I am Luke," I answered.

"We are strangers in your city. Jason, the potter, sent me. My friend is very ill. Will you please let us in and see what you can do for him?"

"I'll be right down."

I hurried down the stairs and unbarred the door. The light from my lamp revealed a tall young man. He was grey with fatigue, and his face was lined with worry. I ushered them into the house, closed the door, and dropped the bar back in place.

Turning, I could see the face of the other man better. His head, large for his stature, hung heavily, drooped to the side. His eyes were half closed, and his mouth sagged. His breathing was shallow. When I touched him, his skin was burning with fever.

"How long has he had this fever?" I queried.

"It comes and goes. When it comes he becomes irrational."

"When did he become ill?" I asked, as I checked his fever.

"Two Sabbaths ago," was the reply.

"Where were you when he became ill?"

"Perga."

"And you traveled all the way from there to Antioch?" I asked incredulously, irritated to think of the ordeal a man as ill as this had been forced to endure to make such a journey. Perga was at least three days' journey for a strong man.

"We were told to get to higher ground where he might recover."

"Who are you?" I asked.

"I am Barnabas," the giant of a man said, "and this is Paul, once known as Saul. We are on a sacred journey."

— — —

That is how I first met Paul—in Antioch, the city located high upon the plains of Pamphilia, near the beautiful Lake Eyerdir that lies like a reflecting pool at the base of the mountains stretching southward into Phrygia. According to tradition, Seleucus—while sacrificing on the hill Silpius—saw an eagle carry the flesh of the offering to the top of Silpius on the south side of the river. He took this as an omen and ordered five or six thousand Athenians and Macedonians to convey the stones and timber that were needed to build the city of Antioch. Seleucus named it for his father.

It became an important commercial center, located on two trade routes. The first leads from Jerusalem, through Antioch of Pisidia, past Troas, and up through the mountain passes to Antioch. From there it goes to

Macedonia and eventually ends in Rome. Many traders pass with their caravans, laden with treasures from the Far East. Roman legions come along this highway, too, on their way from one post to another or just patrolling the way.

The second route comes into the city from the south, beginning in the pesthole of Perga, a seaport town. Here caravans pick up the exotic goods that are headed toward Capadocia, Galatia, and Bithynia.

I call Perga a "pesthole" because there is an influx from there into Antioch. Many of these persons suffer from ague, that debilitating disease characterized by undulant fevers that, if not treated early, can be fatal.

At Alexandria I studied to become a physician under Stratonicus—a very exacting teacher. I thought he was too harsh at the time, but my opinion changed when I began to practice on my own. His ability as a diagnostician rubbed off on me. The many travelers who come through Antioch bring with them diseases and afflictions of a wider range than experienced in most other cities. Thus, I have gained a reputation as a diagnostician among my colleagues. Because of this reputation I met Paul, who was to become my dearest friend.

I wish you could have met him—I believe you would have become his friend, too. Even as I think of him now, my being is filled with a sense of the rightness of things, though I certainly did not feel that way before I came to know him. And I must admit there is still plenty of reason to cry out against injustice, debauchery, cruelty, and corruption in high places. But because of my association with Paul, I know that ultimate rightness will prevail, and I can live with hope and expectation. Becoming his friend meant embracing the magnificent obsession that carried him from one end of the empire to the other in a quest to enlighten lives.

Paul was a man of strong convictions. There is nothing wrong with having convictions. Without them life is dull, but they need a good foundation. If they are based on superstition or tradition, or depend on unseen powers and feelings, they tend to become harsh and inflexible. Persons holding to such convictions tend to persecute anyone who opposes them. Of such are mobs made. Paul faced many radical groups of this kind.

— — —

It is interesting how our friendship developed. After I had examined Paul carefully I began to question Barnabas, since Paul was too weak to talk coherently.

They had joined a caravan and started their journey to Antioch when Paul became ill. His fever would be high one day and break the next, but each bout left him weaker and weaker. He became unable to eat. They had to stop so often that the caravan went on without them. That was when Barnabas had begun carrying his friend. Now he was exhausted also.

I was certain that Paul was suffering from ague. His heartbeat was rapid but weak. The undulant fever was a strong symptom. The green-scummed, stagnant waters of Perga, with their attendant vapors, had struck him down.

Through the night I plied him with fever-fighting herbs and bathed him with tepid water. Barnabas sank into sleep across the room.

When the first rays of the sun explored the treetops, my patient's eyes opened. His fever had abated. I offered him a cup of herb tea.

He accepted it, then paused to search my face. "Are you the physician?" he asked.

"Yes," I replied. "I am Luke and a physician."

"I have been ill," he commented, almost with a sense of wonder. "I have dreamed," he continued. "In it I saw you as one sent from heaven to minister to me."

I listened. My training told me that his dreams were but the delirium that accompanies ague. But in spite of this, I felt he was speaking of something far more profound than that of the physical world.

"Barnabas brought you to me. Your fever had mounted, and he felt it wise to find a physician," I explained.

"Ah!" Paul exclaimed. "But not just any physician. The God of Abraham, Isaac, and Jacob led him to you. Of this I am certain."

His head began to sag as the potion began to take effect. He spoke slowly and almost as one in a trance.

"I am on a holy mission. I must be about my Lord's business . . ."

The words tapered off, and he slipped into deep sleep.

I awakened Barnabas.

"How far is it to Jason's house?" I asked.

"Not far," was his reply.

"Will they take him in for a while?" I asked, nodding toward the sleeping patient.

"Yes. They have already so indicated." He paused and then continued. "I will go and get help. We can carry him on a litter."

"That would be best," I agreed.

Barnabas left after placing his hand upon my shoulder and looking deep into my eyes. "May God watch over you and give you peace," he said.

— — —

By the time he returned, Porphia, my housekeeper, had risen and was busily engaged in preparing my

17

breakfast. Barnabas refused to eat, saying that he would eat at Jason's. He was accompanied by a strapping youth. They placed Paul on a litter, then strode out the door and down the street.

I turned back to the table. Porphia placed a dish of porridge before me. As I ate, she made my bed.

"If someone comes, I'll call," she said as she left the room. She spoke with the crude dialect of the north, for she had come from Bithynia. A woman of deep feelings and unquestioned loyalty, she had been with me for nearly three years. My friend Barsipias first introduced her to me. His brother's wife had come from a small Bithynian village. They had been with Porphia and her parents when they were caught in an avalanche, the aftermath of a storm in the mountains. Digging frantically through the rubbish, they found Porphia, bruised and battered, but alive. Her parents were never seen again, probably buried deep beneath the earth and rocks that filled the gorge. Barsipias and his wife took Porphia into their home and cared for her, but being poor people they could not afford to keep her indefinitely.

Porphia was aware of the problem and tried to the best of her ability to make life easier. She never complained about any of the hard tasks that needed to be done, and often worked long past nightfall. But the lot of an orphan, especially one who is blossoming into womanhood, is not an easy one. There are those who believe that orphans and fatherless children are fair prey to the depravity of lewd men.

It was at this time in her life that Porphia was introduced to me by my friend. I looked at her and saw an attractive young woman, well-favored in womanly graces. Her raven hair shone in the light, a setting for her fair skin. She stood slightly shorter than many—a bit stocky but not obese. When she looked at me, it was an honest look; she did not pretend to false modesty but showed her natural curiosity about someone she had never met before. I liked her.

That evening, as Barsipias and I sat before the fire, we spoke of Porphia. It was then that he told me of his apprehensions as to her safety. "She is ripe for someone to entice her and lead her astray. My wife has warned her of these dangers, and we cannot help worrying about her."

"She seems to be intelligent," I remarked.

"Yes, she is quick to learn. I cannot recall a time that I have had to instruct her more than once in any task."

"I am in need of a housekeeper," I offered. "My work is growing more strenuous and demands most of my time. It would relieve me if I had someone to take care of the house and my meals. Do you think she might be interested?"

Barsipias sat quietly for a bit, then replied, "I don't know. I think that would have to be up to her. We will miss her in our home, but we realize, too, that she needs to be on her own."

"If it is all right with you, I will approach her about it in the morning," I said.

It was agreed. We retired shortly afterward.

The next morning I spoke to Porphia. I told her of my home in Antioch and of my need for help. "My work is so demanding that I do not take the time to provide myself with good meals. Barsipias tells me that you can cook well."

She nodded, modestly.

I continued, "If you would care to do so, I would like to have you come to Antioch to work for me—to care for my house, prepare meals, and do the shopping. I have an upper room that could be yours."

19

As we talked further her enthusiasm for the job grew. I could see it in her eyes and by the animation of her conversation. Before the day was over, it had been decided that she would accompany me back to Antioch. The wages were to be her room and board. Barsipias' wife insisted that I include a clothing allowance—something I had never heard of before, but, as I gave it some thought, I realized that it was not a bad idea.

I have never been sorry for my decision to bring Porphia into my household. She has been a help in more ways than I had imagined. As she became familiar with the routine, I found her interest in my work drew her into my receiving room. Ultimately, I began to use her to help me in treating patients. She grasped ideas quickly and never seemed to forget anything she had once been shown or told.

I finished the meal and, like a puppy with a full stomach, I felt weariness creep into my bones. I went to my room, fell upon the bed, and was asleep in a few minutes.

How long I slept, I do not know, but welling up into my consciousness came the words, "I am on a holy mission!" These words of Paul kept coming to me. I did not feel troubled, but I was curious. I had never met a man who proclaimed himself as sent of God. Though I attended the synagogue of the Jews in Antioch and had accepted Jehovah as God, I did not observe all of the feast days. There always seemed to be a barrier between Luke, the believer, and the devout Jews. When I had talked to Paul, though, he seemed wiser than the rabbis I had met; there did not seem to be such a barrier. It was as if he had known me always, and I felt that I could learn much from him.

At one point I awakened, sat straight up in my bed,

and said, "A holy mission? What is that and what does it mean?" Even as I said the words, a peace came over me, and I knew that all of my questions would be answered. I lay back down and slept again, undisturbed.

The sun had reached its zenith before I awoke again. In spite of the interruptions in my sleep, I felt rested. I was keenly conscious of the puzzle that had faced me during the night, but hope bubbled up inside me as I felt assured the answer was forthcoming. I was no longer troubled by my inability to explain my strange encounter with Paul, yet I was restless, anxiously awaiting my next encounter with him. I was going to go to the home of Jason, the potter, but this would be for more than to visit a patient. I was going to learn what it was that sent these men on a "holy mission."

— — —

I saw several patients that afternoon. Then, as the sun began to lower in the heavens, I made my way to check on Paul.

Barnabas met me in front of the house.

"He is still sleeping but the fever has not returned."

"Has he awakened at any time?" I asked.

"Yes, twice. He asked for water and then went back to sleep," Barnabas replied.

I nodded. The potion I had given him was acting well.

"That is good," I said. "I am glad he is resting. He should be waking up soon again. Then I shall check him."

When we entered the room, Jason was beside Paul, who was still asleep.

"We will be in the garden," Barnabas said to Jason. "Let us know when he starts to awaken."

Jason nodded, and we passed on into the garden area.

There we sat beneath a tree, enjoying its shade and the slight breeze that wafted through the trees, rustling the leaves slightly.

The woman of the house came with a tray of food and a jar of wine. We talked as we ate.

"How did you happen to come to Antioch by way of Perga?" I asked.

Barnabas paused a moment, then spoke.

"We had been on the isle of Cyprus. While there, we met with the governor who had suggested that we take our message to the Galatians. He had many friends there with whom he wanted us to share our message."

"Your message?" I queried.

"Yes . . . but I can see you have not heard of us. We are followers of Jesus Christ, the Messiah." Warming to the subject, he continued. "You are a believer?"

"Yes. Though I am a Greek, I have been a member of the congregation of the synagogue. I find their God to be more attractive to me than the multiplicity of sensuous and cantankerous gods of Rome or Greece."

"Then you know the words that foretell the coming of the Anointed One."

"I have heard them speak of such a hope. He is supposed to rescue them from the oppressors and bring a time of peace."

"You have heard well," Barnabas continued. "We are heralds of the fact that he has come."

Before he could say more, Jason announced, "He is awake."

"Good," I replied.

We went into the house. Paul was still reclining on the pallet. I went to his side and knelt there.

"How do you feel?" I asked.

"I feel much better," he said. "But I am very weak."

"That is to be expected," I assured him. I felt his

brow. There was no fever. Rechecking my diagnosis, I asked, "Have you had any vomiting?"

"No."

"Has there been diarrhea?" I asked, probing his abdomen for possible tumor. There appeared to be none. No vomiting—that eliminated cholera.

Paul shook his head to my question concerning diarrhea.

"Headaches?" I queried.

"Yes."

"Severe?"

"Sometimes."

My diagnosis was confirmed. I spoke to Paul. "Your symptoms often are found in people who have been in Perga. It is well that you have sought higher ground, thus escaping the evil vapors of that swampland.

"You will be ill for several weeks. The fevers come and go about every other day. Even after you become stronger you must be very careful that you do not become chilled or overheated. I have prepared some herbs. A pinch of these in cold water will help control the fever. Drink much water to wash away the cause of the disease."

I turned to Barnabas and Jason. "If the fever mounts, bathe him in tepid water. It will feel cool to him. Do not use cold water, for the shock will cause the fever to grip him more."

All the time I was examining him, Paul watched me searchingly, but he said not a word.

When I had come to know him better, I realized this was unusual. Paul usually dominated any conversation—not in an obnoxious way but by the very strength of his personality. But now he was quiet, trusting, and accepting. Even when I gave him the herbal potion to drink, though he grimaced at the taste, he took it all.

I had mixed in with it some herbs to make him sleep. Soon his eyes closed, and he rested.

I was reluctant to leave. Barnabas' declaration in the garden interested me. What about the Anointed One to be called the Messiah? I wanted to hear more.

Barnabas invited me to accompany him to the garden. He led the way, and I followed.

— — —

The sun had set. We were beginning a new day. It was still light enough that we could see. Once more the good woman of the house brought us food and drink. As the chill of the evening began to creep around us, Barnabas lit a fire on the raised spot in the middle of the garden. Soon the warmth reached out and drew us about it. We sat, resting. The food was satisfying.

In this relaxed atmosphere, I turned to Barnabas and said. "Before we went in, you spoke of the fact that the Messiah had come. And before that, Paul said that you were on a holy mission. I gather that these statements are related, and the thought intrigues me. Tell me more."

While I spoke Barnabas' eyes were fixed upon me. He sank on his elbow, still chewing his food. He reached over, drew his cup to him, and drank. During this time he said not a word, but I could tell his mind was active. I waited expectantly.

Then he began. "Both Paul and I were born in Tarsus. My family moved to Jerusalem when I was a stripling. My father was in the import business, making many trips down to Joppa and back. When he died, I inherited the business. It flourished. I bought much land. I gained great wealth.

"Paul came to Jerusalem several years after we did. A deeply religious man, he studied under Gamaliel and after his marriage was selected to serve in the Sanhedrin. His keen mind and devotion to the law and the traditions of our fathers soon won him respect as one who remembered the ancient landmarks."

As Barnabas talked, I got the picture of a man capable of intense devotion, whether it be to a cause or to a person. Though short and stocky, he was still a man of great strength, able to stand up to whatever life handed out.

Barnabas continued, "When the Nazarene, Jesus, came teaching the truths that had long been lost in the traditions of our people, I found myself greatly attracted to him. Though he broke with some of the sacred traditions, never once did he do injustice to the law of God.

"After much prayer and fasting, I joined with the disciples of Jesus. After his death and resurrection, I sold my house and business and laid the money at the feet of the apostles for use by the church. I began preaching wherever I could, trying to get the Jews to realize that their Messiah had come."

"Ho!" I exclaimed. "This is too fast for me. You speak of the Messiah and Jesus of Nazareth as one. Are they the same?"

"They are the same."

"But you say Jesus died and was resurrected. Death! Resurrection! Messiah!" I exclaimed. This man spoke of strange things. I had seen many who had died, but never had one of them been resurrected. Was this man mad?

Patiently Barnabas paused in his narration to help me understand.

"The prophet Daniel told us of the plan of God whereby the dead shall live. He said, 'Many of them that sleep in the dust of the earth shall awake, some to everlasting life, and some to shame and everlasting contempt. And they that be wise shall shine as the brightness of the firmament; and they shall turn many to righteousness as the stars forever and ever.'

"And did not Hosea say, 'After two days will he revive us; in the third day he will raise us up, and we shall live in his sight.'

"Luke, my friend, the Messiah for whom we have looked for so long has come in the power of heaven, and though men—in order to preserve their traditional ways and in spite of the evidence from on high—did slay him, it did not stop the hand of God. On the third day, he *was* raised up. There were many who saw him and testify even today that he returned from the grave and lives."

"Did you see him?" I asked.

"No, I did not see him. But I have heard the testimony of those who did. They are honest people, and I believe them."

This was heady stuff for me. Never before had I had my religious beliefs challenged. My following of the faith of the Jews had satisfied me as a good way to live, but what I liked I practiced, and what I disliked I ignored. Now I faced something that made me want to accept the prophetic utterances of men long dead to be applicable to my day. It was as if truth came forth from the dust. I had to know more.

"Please go on," I begged.

I don't know whether Barnabas sensed the turmoil within my breast, but it seemed as if his voice took on a different timbre as he continued.

"It was at this very point that Paul and I were unable to agree. He argued that, according to the law, anyone hanged upon a tree was accursed. By such reasoning, he denied the messiahship of Jesus, whom the Romans had crucified. Soon our disagreement became so bitter that our friendship ceased.

"Paul became a sworn enemy of those who taught the teachings of Jesus. Though members of the Sanhedrin had been stripped of their power of capital punishment, its judicial power among the Jews on matters of idolatry, false prophets, and blasphemy extended to wherever Jews lived. The Roman law was quite flexible when it came to application in outlying areas, and the leaders in the Sanhedrin where able to capitalize on this by means of suborned witnesses. Charges often were brought that led to the death penalty under the Roman edict.

"Paul's zeal in seeking out those who actively taught the teachings of Jesus was encouraged by other members of the body. He was sent far and wide to bring back before the tribunal anyone accused of being a teacher of blasphemy.

"But again God was to show his power. Two events were to have profound effect on Paul's life: the stoning of Stephen, and a fateful trip to Damascus."

On into the night Barnabas talked. I was so caught up with his narration that I felt as if I were a part of the events of which he spoke.

He told of Stephen whose wisdom was beyond his years. He told of how this young man had been condemned to death for blasphemy, and of how Paul had been present at the stoning.

It was Stephen's manner of dying that was to haunt Paul the rest of his life. Paul had allowed people to lay their garments at his feet while they went about their grisly task of stoning Stephen. But their victim died with a prayer on his lips for those who caused his death. "Lord, lay not this sin to their charge." It was as if Stephen directed his prayer on Paul's behalf. He who had raised his hand to vote against the man in the Sanhedrin and even worse, stood to watch him die. That white face, marked again and again with the bruising stones, would haunt him in nightmares. And he would cry out in his sleep as those beautiful eyes would turn to look at him and he would hear the words, "Lord, lay not this sin to their charge."

The second event happened when Paul was en route to Damascus. There, on that high road, Paul was brought to the feet of the Lord Jesus. The details of this were given me at a later time when Paul told me his own story. But even then, as Barnabas related these events, I found myself experiencing vicariously a movement in my life that made me know I could never be satisfied until I knew all I could about this man and his Savior.

Barnabas continued his narration, and I listened.

"It was in Damascus that Paul was turned about, and though I heard the story of his conversion told by those who came to Jerusalem, it was not until three years later that I saw my friend's face again.

"Paul came to Jerusalem, fleeing his former friends who now believed him to be a traitor to Judaism. But he found it hard to make friends in Jerusalem, for he was still remembered as a hard man, quick to anger, slow to forgive, obstinate, and short on charity. It was hard for many to believe this man had changed so greatly.

"I guess I was the one who opened the way for him. I sensed the change in him. And when we met, it was Paul who fell on his face and begged my forgiveness for the harsh words he had spoken to me when we had parted. I reached down and helped him to his feet. Then, standing there, I embraced him as a brother with such emotion that all who observed knew that I wholeheartedly accepted him. Slowly the others began to listen to his story of his experience with Jesus, for he felt that his was just as valid and personal as the experiences of the disciples who walked with the Lord."

By now the first streaks of dawn were beginning to show along the eastern horizon. The occasional twitter of birds could be heard as they began to awaken. We had talked the whole night through, but I was not tired. It seemed as if I had a renewed strength in my body, and that this day would be one of the best of my life.

— — —

Porphia was already up when I arrived home. Used to my being away—often all night as I tended the sick—she asked, "How is your patient?"

"He is going to be all right," I replied. But not wanting to leave it at that, I continued: "He is a very strange man. And his companion is like him. I have never met anyone else who affected me as they do."

Porphia paused in her housework to look inquiringly at me, but said nothing.

"They tell me of a man named Jesus, a Nazarene, whom they claim is the promised Messiah," I went on.

"I know nothing of such things," she said as she turned back to her work.

"Ah, Porphia," I cried. "It is not so much what they say but how it has affected their lives. They have become extraordinary men whose lives are dedicated to a great cause."

"Great causes get men killed," was her reply.

Yes, that was an astute remark. Did not such a great cause bring death to Jesus? I turned, pondering my newfound concepts, wondering where they might lead if I followed them as I was inclined to do.

Chapter 2

The next two weeks passed quickly. My days were filled with tending my patients. My nights were spent with Barnabas and Paul.

Paul grew stronger and participated more in our conversations. As he did, I found myself falling under the spell of his personality. The latent energy in this man began to show, but there was something more than just his vitality or my medical skills working in him. His recovery was so rapid that I marveled. My experience with ague was that it took months for a patient as ill as Paul had been to regain his strength, but he was already sitting up most of the day. And in spite of my warnings, he spent hours at night talking about his religion. Often I was present. The things he said began to make sense to me.

"God has created us for his own divine purpose," he said on one occasion. "It is up to us to become one with him in order to understand that purpose. That is the only way we will fully mature."

I liked that.

I was astounded at his knowledge. He was well versed in the ancient prophets, but he taught as no rabbi did.

And Barnabas—as landowner and man of business he had had no time for the scholar's role, but his knowledge was vast. On one occasion he had amazed me. I had asked him to explain how Jesus could truly be the expected Anointed One.

Little did I realize what I had let myself in for! As if he had led me to this moment, Barnabas, with a delighted gleam in his eyes, began to unfold the story of Jesus to me.

When Herod was the king of Judea, many strange things happened. Some of the great prophecies began to be fulfilled.

Malachi had said, "Behold, I will send you Elijah the prophet before the coming of the great and dreadful day of the Lord; and he shall turn the heart of the fathers to the children, and the heart of the children to their fathers, lest I come and smite the earth with a curse."

Barnabas said John the Baptist was the Elijah sent as a forerunner of the coming of the Anointed One. He told how Zacharias sired John through Elizabeth, daughter of Aaron. He expanded with how an angel had told Zacharias of the mission of his son; though Elizabeth was beyond the years of children, she bore John.

About the same time a young woman, Mary—espoused to a man named Joseph—had a strange experience with an angel. She was told that she would bear a child, though she had never been with a man. It was further explained to her that her son was the expected Messiah and that the power of God would cause this to come to pass. It did.

This was an incredible story being told to me by my new-found friend, but because of the spirit about him and something that touched my very soul, I found myself believing him.

Within my breast a burning desire to know more was kindled. The years of study at Alexandria and all of the knowledge I had gleaned from the library at the Temple of Serapes, combined with the many hours spent at the feet of Stratonicus, had filled me with the knowledge of insignificant things compared with the life-centered, down-to-earth insights these two men gave me.

I departed reluctantly. There were patients waiting to see me—one with tenesmus and another with ozena. Also, there were a number of simple cases of inflamation.

But I knew I would return that evening. I wanted to hear what Paul had to say.

When I arrived at home Porphia met me at the door. Her face was drawn. Her hands fluttered like the wings of an injured bird. Being a stoic person, she was not easily upset. Something was wrong to agitate her so.

She reached out, grabbed my hand, and began leading me into the house. "Come," she said, with such emphasis it carried the tone of a command. I followed her into my reception room. There, writhing on the floor was a young woman. Her body was wracked with spasms so great that her heels drummed an uneven beat on the floor, and her head—being held by a tearful man—strained to and fro until it was all he could do to keep her from beating it on the floor. The violence of her spasms could be seen in the straining muscles of the man's arms as he sought to hold her.

Her face was contorted until it looked like the visage of a demon-god, often sculptured in stone at barbarian shrines. A bloody froth forced its way between her clinched teeth and dribbled down upon her breast. Deep groans of anguish welled up in her throat, the sounds of a soul in torment.

A second man knelt at he feet, and when her body spasmed most violently, he would throw his arms about her legs in an attempt to lessen the damage caused when she tossed herself about on the floor.

The older of the two—the one holding her head—looked up at me. Tears ran down his cheeks. His voice faltered, then came with strength. "Oh, sir! this is my daughter. The demons have taken over her body and are destroying her. Please, can you help her?"

His plea was touching. The young man at her feet—perhaps her brother—looked toward me expectantly.

I knelt down beside her and placed my hand against the side of her neck. Her pulse was strong but very rapid. I could feel the cords of her neck swell as another paroxysm began. I looked up, caught Porphia's eye, and signaled for her to assist me.

Leaving her to assist in restraining the woman, I hastened to my laboratory and mixed herbs that could cause the patient to relax. The problem would be to feed the mixture to her without strangling her. I took a small amount of the extract of the poppy and rolled it into a ball, then placed it on a stem. Turning to the fireplace, I held it in the flame until it ignited. A whitish smoke began to billow from it. Quickly I returned to the side of the young woman. Gently I blew the smoke toward her nostrils. Her exertions caused her to breathe heavily and soon she had inhaled enough for it to begin to have an effect. Her muscles began to relax, and she became less violent. The demonic mask slipped from her face, and peace began to retore her to her natural state. She was a beautiful woman! Her face was as fair as that of Venus; her lips were full, and her eyelashes long and silky. As Porphia wiped her face with a damp cloth, color began to come back to her skin.

Now, as she lay relaxed on the lap of her father, I pressed the side of her jaws to force her mouth open, and poured the mixture I had prepared between her lips. Her eyes opened as I began and she started to struggle— then settled back and swallowed it all. Soon the elixir began to work. Her eyelids became heavy and her breathing steady. Slowly she sank into deep sleep.

"Take her to the other room," I said to Porphia.

Picking up the young woman in her powerful arms, Porphia carried her through the doorway. I turned to the men, fixing my eye on the father.

"When did this affliction first begin?" I asked.

"Early this morning, before the cock crew," he replied.

"No, I mean when in her life did you first find out that a demon had possessed your daughter?"

"She had seen fourteen summers," was his answer.

"How old is she now?" I queried.

"Eighteen summers," he replied.

Four years, I thought to myself. Four years of this suffering!

The father continued, "At first it seemed to be but a fit of temper. Then we noticed that it came on when she became excited. Now, there seems to be no warning. It comes on quickly, and every time seems to be worse than the one before."

"It follows a pattern I have seen before," I said. "It appears that the demon has had time to possess her thoroughly."

"We took her to the priests at the temple of Diana. They gave us hope, but after spending much of our possessions to pay for the incantations we found that she was no better. In fact, she seems to be getting worse." The father was agonizing over his daughter. It was as if her suffering was his.

"We had hoped that you might be able to treat her," the brother said. "Someone told us that you had great experience."

Ah, how that might have filled me with pride a few weeks ago. But after meeting Paul and hearing his story from Barnabas, I had become aware that I was not nearly the learned physician that I had thought. I had seen and heard things that were beyond all of my learning.

"Yes, I have seen such cases before," I said. "Persons can be possessed by one or more demons. The effects differ according to the individual, but they all have certain common traits. The person is possessed slowly, as if the

34

demon is trying out his power. The condition always gets worse until those who are possessed either die from malnutrition—not being able to eat—or throw themselves over some cliff to their death."

"Is there no hope?" asked the father.

"I would do you a disservice if I gave you false hope," I replied. "Sometimes these demons leave the afflicted one as suddenly as they came. But, in all of my practice, I have known of only two such recoveries."

I could see his shoulders sag at my words.

"Let me examine her more carefully," I suggested.

I went into the room where Porphia had taken the woman. She had laid her upon a pallet below a large window where the breezes could blow over her. As I approached the patient, Porphia stood back, watching.

I drew her garment aside and palpitated her body. I listened to the sound of her breathing, felt her pulse, counted her breaths. There was a swelling behind her left ear. At first I thought it might be from her violent threshing upon the floor, but further examination showed it to be of another nature. When I pressed on it, she stirred uneasily. Obviously it was painful.

I sat back. There was something about this young woman that attracted me. It was not sexual attraction, though she was lovely enough to cause most any man to lust after her. There was an aura about her that seemed to speak of basic goodness. I had seen her in the most agonizing condition, face reflecting demonic possession—a most unattractive condition; yet as I looked upon her reclining form, I felt that she was a person of worth. To me came a knowledge that there was a potential in her that transcended all she had ever been allowed to be before, and I found my heart going out to her in a strange way. Always I had kept myself aloof from my patients, for I had learned early that when a physician became emotionally involved with his patients he was not able to care for them as well as he might. That does not mean that I did not care—just that my caring was from a distance that allowed me to be objective.

At this juncture in my musings, Porphia moved to my side. Placing her hand upon my shoulder, she looked down on me as I looked up. Her face was calm, but behind it was a fervency that bespoke of something upon her mind. "What of Paul?" she asked.

"What of him?" I queried. This was such a strange question that I was taken aback. Then it began to dawn on me the drift of her query. She was sensing the same feelings as I was concerning this young woman.

"You told me of his healings," she went on. She was direct and to the point.

"But Porphia," I said, hesitatingly, "the swelling behind this woman's ear speaks of a very serious condition. I have known of such cases and have never seen any healed. Always, it has claimed their lives."

"Is Paul's god impotent?" Porphia's eyes held me in their accusing gleam.

I knew she had taken everything literally when I had told her of the many times that Paul had laid his hands upon persons and they had come away whole. Did I dare hold out this slim hope to these strangers? No, that was not the crux of the matter. Did I dare to offer all that I could?

"Porphia," I said, "It is a matter of faith."

As I looked into her eyes, I knew I was looking at a woman of faith. There shone from her a light such as I had never seen before. I knew then and there that I loved this woman with a depth that would take me a lifetime to fathom. I drew her to me and held her close. It was a magic moment in my life.

Then reality began to force its way back to my mind, and reluctantly I stepped back. She slowly turned, and we both looked down on the sleeping patient. Letting Porphia go, I turned toward the other room.

As I entered the two men looked at me expectantly. How was I to tell them that I could do nothing for their loved one from a physician's viewpoint but could offer them hope through the instrumentality of faith? Never before had I faced this difficult task.

I did not realize at the time what had happened to me. I was too much taken up with the healing of that young woman. But later I was to come to the realization that it was through this experience that I had crossed over from being converted to Judaism to being a follower of the Nazarene. From this day forward, I was a recognized Christian. I had not only come to believe, but I had been a good missionary, for I had told the story so well that Porphia had come to believe, too. And now I was about to bring three more lives in contact with my friend Paul, the results of which could introduce them to the Christian faith as well.

"I have examined your daugher," I said to the father. "Her affliction is a serious one." They waited as I sought to put into words what was in my mind. "As a physician I can do nothing more than I have already done. I could sedate her so the attacks would not affect her, but she would be unable to enjoy life. She would spend all of her time in a stupor."

I could see them crumbling with my pronouncement. "But," I continued, "I have a friend who I believe can help." Should I tell them that he was a Christian? I took the easy way and left that to Paul. "My friend is Paul of Tarsus," I went on. "It happens that he is in our city at this very time. I would like to have him meet your daughter. Perhaps he can help her."

"I want my daughter to be well," the father said, "but I have spent so much that I have little left to pay him."

The son broke in. "If he can cure my sister, I will become his slave and wait upon him the rest of my life."

I was touched deeply by this young man's love for his sister. The life of a slave is not an easy one. He ceases to be a person and becomes but chattel, to be used and sold at his master's whim.

"I will leave that up to Paul," I said.

Then send for him," urged the father. The son nodded in agreement.

I called to Porphia. When she entered the room I said, "Go to the house of Jason. Ask if Paul could come here to meet this woman."

"She is stirring," Porphia offered. "Someone should be with her."

"I will attend her," I replied. "Go quickly."

Porphia slipped into her sandals and was on her way. We went into the room where the young woman lay. Porphia had done wonders with her. Her hair was combed and lay in ringlets about her face. Her eyes were searching the room, and when we entered she turned. Seeing her father, she struggled to rise. Her brother moved quickly to her side. "Julia, lie back and rest. We are here, and all is well."

Though she allowed him to press her back on the bed, she was ill at ease and sought her father's face.

"Papa, where are we?" she asked.

"We are in the house of Luke, the physician, my dear," was his reply.

"I have been sick again?" she asked.

"Yes, dear," he answered, "but you are going to be all right." Turning to me he held out his hand. "Julia, I want you to meet Luke."

"Oh, I remember you. You gave me something to drink." She spoke softly.

"So you could rest."

"I am tired."

"Yes, that is normal."

"Can I go home, now?"

Her father spoke up, "Julia, there is someone else whom we have called to see you."

Her eyes grew large, and she sat upright. "Not another of those horrid priests!" Before anyone could answer, she continued, "They did terrible things to me, Papa. Terrible things." She drew her arms about herself, hunched over, and began crying.

I spoke up. "No, Julia, not one of those. This man is my friend, and I think you will find him to be a friend to you, too."

She looked up at me doubtfully. All of the bad experiences she had in the temple of Diana were flooding through her mind. I knew what she must have feared. I was aware of how the priests prostituted their charges to gain money for the coffers of the temple. Young girls were used in the name of religion to satisfy the lusts of those who came to honor Diana. The despicable practice of using temple maidens was one of the things that had turned me away from that kind of worship.

"Don't be afraid," I assured her. "Paul is a good man."

I told her of how Paul had come into my life, and of the miraculous recovery of this man of God. I related some of the experiences he had shared with me, and how the power of God had moved in the lives of those he had touched.

Almost an hour had passed before we heard footsteps at the door. Porphia had returned with Barnabas and Paul. I arose and went to meet them. After telling of the seizure and of my diagnosis, I explained how I could do no more for her and why I wanted her to meet Paul.

Paul listened attentively, then raised his hand. "But, my friend, God chooses to heal whom he will. It is not by any power of mind that healing comes. It is the measure of faith in God that makes his Spirit able to work its wonders."

"Yes," I replied, "but remember when you told me of how the friends brought a man to Jesus by lowering him through the roof. Whose faith was at work there?"

Paul looked at me searchingly. "I cannot answer that question. All I know is that the man was healed by the power in Jesus."

"Then let us go in to meet this woman. Let your judgment be used to tell whether or not there is faith enough to heal her," I urged.

We went into the room. Julia was sitting upright, her back against the wall, her legs tucked beneath her. Once more I was touched by the basic goodness that shone from her face. As she looked up at us when we entered the room, there was an expression of complete trust. Her body was relaxed. It was then that I felt I had done the right thing in bringing Paul to her.

I approached the father. "Sir," I said, "this is my friend, Paul, of whom I spoke." It dawned on me at this juncture that through all of our recent experiences I had not learned the man's name. He saved me the embarrassment of having to ask by introducing himself.

"I am Achaicus, the artisan," he said. "And this is my son, Appolonius." They bowed to Paul, who returned their salutation.

"I am Paul, born Saul of Tarsus, an apostle of Jesus Christ."

I went on after the introductions. Turning to Julia, I said, "Julia, meet my friend Paul."

Her eyes, already on him, were held by his. Paul reached forth and took her by the hand. She arose and stood before him, her dark hair flowing in curls about her face. Her hand remained in his. There seemed to be a flow of communion between them.

Suddenly, the calm was broken. A subtle change began to occur. Her face went blank, then began to contort. Her limbs grew rigid, then began to convulse. Her hands tore at her dress. She sank on the floor with such suddenness that she slipped out of Paul's grasp. Her head thumped on the hard stones. Julia was seized once more by the demon who possessed her.

I hastened to kneel beside her. Calling to Porphia, "Bring me the opiate," I prepared to administer the medication. Achaicus and Appolonius stood back, but the anguish they felt was graven on their faces.

I felt Paul's hand on my shoulder. "Leave her alone. The Spirit of God moves upon me to administer to her," he said.

I stepped back. Standing over the writhing woman Paul extended his hand, pointed his finger at her, and said in a voice that seemed to penetrate every part of the house: "In the name of Jesus Christ, I adjure you to depart from this woman. Go! Leave her in peace!"

It was as if he spoke to someone other than the woman. I could feel the power of those words as they fell from his lips. And even as I watched, the convulsions increased, beginning at her feet and working upward. Then, with a loud cry in a voice of one in torment and despair, the presence in her departed. I felt as if it were leaving the room.

I stood transfixed, staring. Julia, who had just a moment before worn the mask of demonic possession, now lay relaxed on the floor. The change was dramatic...something I shall never forget.

I looked around the room. Father and son stood together, their arms about one another, staring. Porphia—my stoic Porphia—stood at the doorway, arms folded across her bosom, her face glowing as if this was what she had expected all along.

Paul stooped, took Julia's hand, and drew her to her feet. Once again, her eyes were fixed on his face. "The Lord Jesus Christ has taken mercy on you, my child. In you lies the bud of faith. Go forth whole and fulfill the life he has given you."

Strange words, these. Yet it seemed as if she knew what they meant. She nodded her head, turned, and took her place beside her father.

Suddenly the spell of surprise was over. Achaicus rushed forward and fell to his knees at the feet of Paul. Looking up at him, then bowing his head in humility he said, "Oh, great Paul, you have shown me the power of your God. Diana has been powerless, but your Jesus has all power. Diana was cruel and cared naught for my daughter except for her gratification. Your Jesus has shown mercy on a helpless one and promised her a life worthwhile. Teach me of his ways. My family and I will follow him and worship him forever."

Once again Paul stretched forth his hands as he took Achaicus by the shoulders and lifted him to his feet. "You are perceptive, my son. You know it was by no power of my own that your daughter was delivered from the demonic power. For this I am gratified. Come to the house of Jason this evening, join with us, and learn of Jesus Christ."

It was a matter of some time before Paul was able to get away. After Achaicus and his son and daughter left, he turned to me. "My friend, you have the making of a missionary. Porphia told me of how you had convinced her of the power of God. She has indicated that she wants to join us. Now, through your own faith, three more souls have been added to the flock." His arm went about my shoulders, and he drew me to him with great affection.

I had listened to many things Paul had said, but for some reason these words meant more to me than anything else. I longed to know more of the story of how he had come to be an apostle for Jesus Christ. That night I would join others at the house of Jason to hear his testimony.

Chapter 3

I was late for the meeting at Jason's. Porphia and I had been very busy all afternoon. Some of the citizens of Antioch were assembled at a local inn when a centurian and his men came in. They were in a surly mood, and when they began abusing the innkeeper's daughter, tempers began to mount. A fight broke out. For a while it seemed as if the citizens were going to succeed in ousting the rude soldiers, but the soldiers drew their weapons and inflicted numerous wounds on their opponents. I was called to the inn. After checking the wounded I sent those who could walk to my house for treatment, but I had to care for three of the more grievously injured at the scene. This involved sewing up some gaping wounds and applying bandages to hold the torn flesh together. By the time I had cared for all, it was past dark.

Porphia and I hurried through the dark streets until we arrived at Jason's house. He met us at the door, and we found a place in the back of the room.

Paul was standing before the group. He had introduced Achaicus and his family, after which they had told of their experience in the healing of Julia. It was gratifying to see her seated among the women—her face shining—no longer fearful that she might be stricken again.

Paul spoke. "There are certain men who oppose the work I have been called to do. They have come into nearly every city where I have gone, calling me a traitor to God, a blasphemer. Tonight I want to tell you of my conversion to the way of Jesus. I leave it with you to determine whether or not they have grounds on which to accuse me.

"Though I had heard of Jesus, the Nazarene, whom some called the Anointed One, I think that my hatred of him was blown into full flame with the accusation of Stephen before the Sanhedrin. I served on that body and was one who heard him accuse the Jews of having crucified the Anointed One of God. But it was his claim that he saw Jesus sitting on the right hand of God that truly incensed me.

"Reared a strict Pharisee, I had tried to live up to every precept of Torah.

"On that fateful day we were called to gather at our meeting place. The leader was seated in his usual spot. Seventy of us were ranged about him so when the accused was brought in we completely surrounded him. The accused was a handsome man, in spite of the roughing up he had received at the hand of his captors. His clothes hung in tatters until they barely covered his nakedness.

"We listened to the charges, then we gave him a chance to speak. The words that followed fanned my hatred of the followers of Jesus into white heat: 'Behold, I see the heavens opened, and the Son of man standing on the right hand of God.' Until then I had listened patiently as he rehearsed some of the glories and dark moments of Israel. He was well tutored. He knew the prophets. But when he ascribed equality with God to this Jesus, it was more than I could bear.

"When the time came for the vote, I cast my pebble against him. He was taken from our midst to a place outside to be stoned. So fervent was my feeling in this matter that I followed and even held the cloaks of those who prepared to stone him. I watched with satisfaction as I saw the first bruises forming. Now the rain of stones came fast, and soon he was streaked with blood. Then I saw him lift his face toward the heavens. His words, clear and piercing, fell on my ears. 'Lord, lay not this sin to their charge.' That voice was to haunt me through all of my nights, but I tried to disregard it. I was stung with the accusations of Stephen against not only the judges of the Sanhedrin but all of Judah: 'Ye stiff necked and un-circumcised in heart . . . who have received the law . . . and have not kept it!'

"I went forth to drown that accusation and my un-settling experience of the stoning by persecuting every follower of the sect I could find. If he were a Jew, I haled him before the court for judgment. If he were a Gentile, I sought means of haling him before the Roman authorities on any charge I could find. All I wanted was to rid the earth of this scourge. But I could not get away from the vision of that disquieting face. I could not forget that his prayer was for me . . . it seemed so personal. My guilt made me feel that he had looked deep within me as he died that day.

"So when I had the opportunity to go to Damascus to search out these troublemakers, I welcomed the chance. A change of scenery would be good.

"I look back on that decision as the turning point of my life. The beginning was at the pit where Stephen died. If he had not prayed for me I might never have met my Lord on that hot, dry road outside Damascus.

"At that time, however, I felt I ought to do whatever I could contrary to the name of Jesus of Nazareth. My fame as an inquisitor had gone before me. I was known as one who spared neither man or woman.

"I took the same route that Abraham had taken when he journeyed with his flocks and herds from Hebron into the land of Palestine, except I was traveling in the op-posite direction. Where he had crossed over to found a people, I was to cross over in the opposite direction with the intent to preserve that people.

"Taking the northern road and traveling over the high ridges that lay between the valley of the Jordan and the coastal plains, I recalled the words of the Psalmist as I walked: 'The hills stand about Jerusalem; even so standeth the Lord round about his people, from this time forth forevermore.' I felt that I was the arm of the Lord at this moment.

"We passed through the hills of Samaria, though I would rather have navigated around that accursed people's land; but this was the route the caravan had chosen and I stayed with it. The trip was too dangerous for a man to travel alone. Soon the snow-capped top of Mount Hermon came into view: the tower of Lebanon which looks toward Damascus.

"The tortuous part of the journey was now to begin. After dipping into the valley of the Jordan we traveled along the foothills and the base of Antilibanus. It was so arid the very stones looked thirsty. Plants were sparse and withered. The sun beat down on us with scorching intensity, and I plodded on as if in a daze. Through this desert land we trudged. The snow on Mount Hermon mocked us. We were like men drowning in a dusty sea. This was our sixth day.

"Reaching an eminence we could see Damascus in the distance. But instead of feeling relief and the joy of anticipation, I felt as if the burning from without and within would conquer my spirit. I doubted that I could make this last part of the journey. I was like Moses when he viewed the promised land but was denied entrance. I saw Damascus from afar, but the next events that were to transpire were to deny me the triumphal entry I had anticipated. I was stricken blind!

"From the base of Antilibanus flow fountains of water that are finally swallowed up by the desert sands. These streams from Lebanon were the true treasure of

Damascus, for no city can exist without good water.

"For miles around this oasis gardens of roses, shrubbery, and fruit trees abound. Within the city nearly every dwelling has a fountain. You can go nowhere without hearing the soft murmur of splashing waters. Night lights twinkle from their restless surface.

"All of this I missed at my entry because of the next events. The sun was at its zenith. I was feeling the heat of that orb and had retreated beneath my cloak. Suddenly a great light shone round about me. Never had I seen such brilliance. It was brighter than the sun but not as hot. It was so powerful a force that my garment was ripped from my shoulders. Even so, it lifted the oppressive heat from my body. This was replaced with a new kind of burning—within my breast. So sudden and intense was it that I became terrified—as were my companions. We fell to the ground, but try as we might we could not escape that light from heaven. Confusion reigned among us.

"Then something began to happen within me. The light seemed to set my soul on fire, and I heard a voice. In pure, clear Hebrew the message came: 'Saul, Saul, why persecutest thou me?'

"An awful dread clutched my breast. I was afraid and dared not look. Standing before me was a man. His raiment was as the whitest snow. His arms were bare, and in his hands were the print of nails. It was from him that the light shown. His face revealed an inner sadness—as if he bore the woes of the world. His eyes penetrated me, searching my soul. I was undone. I knew this was Jesus of Nazareth. More than this, I knew of a truth that he was the Anointed One, the Messiah for whom I had looked all my life.

"He continued: 'It is hard for thee to kick against the goad.'

"Oh, what terror filled my soul. What could I say to the Messiah whom I had denied? I stammered, 'Who art thou, Lord?' Yet I knew the answer.

"'I am Jesus whom thou persecutest,' he said. Then he repeated, 'It is hard for thee to kick against the goad.'

"Then I knew! All of my life had been directed toward this moment when I should come face to face with my Lord. The goad of God had directed my footsteps. In my self-righteousness I had rebelled. No longer could I do so. All of the hatred drained out of me. I was left weak. My sight turned inward as I cried, 'What will you have me do?'

"If he had said that I should throw myself from a high hill, I would have done so. But that was not what he wanted.

"'Arise, and go into the city, and it shall be told thee what thou must do.'

"Even as I stared, the light faded away. Though there was light within me and the vision of Jesus was clear, I was blind to all about me. I was blind to the world.

"I could hear the voices of my companions as they tried to sort out what had happened. None had heard the voice. Some said they heard a rumbling. Others claimed the wind had sounded. But I knew the sound was for me. My life was being turned around.

"I was led into the city by my wondering and confused traveling companions. The persecuting lion had become a meek lamb. They took me to the house of Judas where I was given a room. There I sat, waiting.

"The good woman of the house tended me with much clucking of the tongue. She sought to cool my brow with wet cloths. She brought me food, but I was being fed by food she knew not of. I was not depressed. The loss of sight was a boon because it shut out distractions so my mind could feed on all I had been taught before and on what I had heard of this man, Jesus. I sat waiting for the Lord to tell me what else I was to do. This was my first lesson in faith. I had no doubt that God could do as he wished. But I was to learn that he can use people for his purposes. Though I had read of the prophets, they remained distant from my time. Their day was past, I had been taught. It took a visitation during the night hours to show that they still lived. Jesus appeared again. This time he told me to expect a man named Ananias who would bring me a message.

"Three days passed after the visitation. It was late evening when there was a knock on the door. The lady of the house opened to a man of mature years, 'Is this the house of Judas?' he asked.

"'Yes,' she replied.

"'Is this where Saul of Tarsus resides?' he queried.

"'He abides here.'

"'I have been sent to bring him a message,' he stated.

"I was straining to hear the conversation. I knew this was my messenger. I leaped to my feet and stood. 'Let him in,' I cried.

"She opened the door wider, and he came into the room. 'I am Ananias, a disciple of Jesus the Christ,' he announced. He came to where I stood and placed his hand on my shoulder. I bowed my head to acknowledge him and softly said. 'I have been waiting for you.'

"He continued, 'I was praying in my room when I was taken up in a vision of the Lord. He carried me away in the Spirit and showed me this house. He said that he had prepared you for my coming. I am to lay my hands upon your head for a blessing.'

"Gently he pressed me down to my knees. I heard him taking something from his girdle, and I caught the scent of oil. He anointed my head. Gently placing his hands on it he said, 'Saul, in the name of Jesus Christ, having been commissioned by him, I place my hands upon your head to bring you the blessing of healing. The Lord has chosen you as one of his vessels and commissions you to prepare yourself to go forth among the Gentiles, as well as the children of Israel, so all may know his name. You shall suffer many things for his name's sake, but you shall stand before rulers and kings to bear your testimony. And now, O Lord, send thy promised Spirit upon this man, Saul, to heal his blindness, both of body and of spirit, that he may be a whole soul in thy service.'

"At the completion of those words and the removal of his hands, I felt as if a curtain had been lifted from before me. The light burst through, and I could see Ananias' face.

"The disciples were afraid of me at first, but as the weeks went by, they accepted me. It was from their lips I began to learn the wonderful words that Jesus taught. My life took on a new set of values.

"I shall never regret the years I spent at the feet of Gamaliel, but I know now that all of my learning of the past was but a preparation for this greater truth. The traditions and legalisms took on new meaning. Life became dynamic. The ancient past and the expectancies that grew out of them were washed in a new color. I came to know that throughout all time, God is truly in charge. His inexorable purpose has not and never can be denied. People are God's instruments—glorious instruments.

"The prophets took on a new dimension, also. Once I had felt their utterances were exclusively for the benefit of the Hebrews. Keeping Torah required living according to the traditions of the fathers. Every moment of every day was filled with rules, regulations, and practices that made us pawns in the hand of God. Now I saw the function of the law and the prophets was to free all people to rise above the bonds of legalism to the greater law of consequence. Punishment and retribution from a vengeful God were a distortion of truth. Instead, there is a more exacting understanding through the law of love and the acceptance of the consequences of action.

"These truths came fast, crowding in on my consciousness. I thrilled with the vibrant understanding that my old learnings were now directed into a whole new way of life. With such understanding came a kind of freedom that bound at the same time. I was freed to the law of love and goodness but bound to live it as well, for there was no other way. Oh, how I longed to tell my friends of what I had learned! My heart was with the Jews. They had looked for so long for the Anointed One. Now that he had come, once more they could gather into one place and become a nation of the Lord.

"One Sabbath I made my way to the synagogue at Damascus. When the time came for expounding on the scripture I, as a visitor from Jerusalem and emissary of the Sanhedrin, was extended the privilege to speak. I arose, stood before them, and spoke; 'Ye men of Israel, hear me. Long have we suffered because of the sins of our fathers. In the wilderness our fathers wandered for forty years. But God has always been mindful of us. He drove out the seven nations in Caanan. He gave us judges in our time of need. But still our people had no peace. Always, we have awaited the time when God would act and return to us the glory of the past when David reigned. We have looked for the Anointed One of Israel.'

"I could tell that they were listening carefully. A murmur spread throughout the synagogue, and I continued; 'You will recall John the Baptizer. Recall that there were those who would have declared him the one. But he said it was not so. He proclaimed there was one coming after him. I know that his testament was true, for I have met the Messiah. I am here today to declare that the Anointed One has come. He is Jesus of Nazareth, the one whom the Jerusalem Jews caused to be slain.'

"I did not get to go further. There was an angry sound that began with the leaders of the synagogue and then swept through the congregation. The cry of 'Traitor' came from some. In their anger, I was shoved out of the synagogue and, if I had not been borne away by my friends, my life might have ended there.

"Such has been my fate in whatever synagogue I appear; but in each place there are a few who seek me out and listen in the quiet of my abode. I have longed to tell the Jews that their Messiah has come, but they will not hear me.

"My life was in danger at Damascus. My friends sought to protect me. At the next meeting of the elders, it was suggested that I go into Arabia for a time of meditation and prayer. In this place I would have time to think and to try these ideas where I was not known."

— — —

The testimony of Paul continued. On the very next day he left for Arabia. He trudged southward along the route Moses had taken. For safety he traveled with caravans from one town to the next. Among these people whose peripetetic way of life kept them moving to where their flocks could feed, Paul's trade of tent-maker was in demand. He always found work for his hands—either repairing a worn tent or putting a new one together. He never wanted for food.

As he worked, his mind was busy, too. His day began with prayer. The essence of every prayer was: "Lord, here I am. Speak to me that I may know how to do your will. Teach me, that I may teach."

Slowly there developed within him a sense of destiny. He knew that he would be thrust back into the midst of controversy soon. This was his time of preparation. And as he prepared, he was busy sharing his ideas and his faith with all who would listen while he worked.

God, who in times past had led the Jews and preserved them from the misfortunes of war and pestilence, was now moving among all people with a message. It was beginning to dawn on Paul what his first call in Damascus had meant. The Gentiles listened when he spoke.

At last he settled in the city of Succoth, on the edge of the land of Goshen. For two years he remained at this crossroad where travelers came and went daily. Caravans were outfitted for their long journey across the desert, or unloaded their cargo for transport to the seacoast towns. Paul's reputation as a craftsman spread. By this time he had worked out a routine. Early in the morning he arose and went out to pray. The Spirit of the Lord often encompassed him, and it seemed as if he was being taught at the feet of Jesus, even as Peter, James, and John had been. His mind was quickened with new insights. At times he was so overcome that he lay prostrate on the ground while the Spirit nurtured him. When he arose, he was refreshed.

After his return to the shop, sitting crosslegged with tent material piled around him, he talked with the people who gathered to hear the story of Jesus of Nazareth. Many tarried to ask questions—and to test him.

One afternoon a man who came to listen remained long after the others had left. Paul looked toward him questioningly. The man said, "I wish that Jesus of yours would come to this place."

"Why?" asked Paul.

"Well, you tell how he healed the sick," was the reply.

"Do you need healing?" asked Paul.

"It is my daughter. From birth she has been afflicted. At first we did not know anything was wrong, but then we began to realize that something was amiss. She would sit for hours and not respond to anything we would say. It was as if she were not present. This becomes worse as she grows older." The man put his hands to his face, and tears dripped through his fingers as he sobbed. "I wish Jesus would come to my house."

Paul sat quietly, but his spirit was carried away. He did not move. He said nothing. Then slowly, as if afraid, he said, "Bring your daughter to me."

The man left. At sundown he returned. With him was a demure girl of about twelve years. Though she came with her father, the vacant stare in her eyes told that she was living in her own world.

Paul fixed his eyes on her, but there was no sign of recognition. After a few minutes, however, she turned her head toward him, and her eyes met his. They continued in this manner for several more minutes. Finally Paul spoke. "Come closer, little one." He patted a place on the tent cloth where he was working.

She paused for a moment, then with her eyes still fixed on him, she seated herself where he had indicated.

"What is your name?" Paul asked, as he pulled and straightened the cloth.

The girl reached out, picked up a piece of the material, and absently began to follow his movements. "I am called Elana," she said in a voice so low as to almost be inaudible. Her speech was slow and measured.

Paul talked with her, telling what he was doing. He compared the material to people's lives. He spoke of the power of God to take lives that were fragmented and put them together again. He spoke of love and power.

The girl watched as his hands moved skillfully over the tenting. She seemed fascinated. The father stood in awe, for this was the first time she had seemed interested in anything others were doing.

A strange feeling came over Paul. He felt compassion for the girl—but something more was moving upon him. It seemed as if a great cloak was being placed upon his shoulders. With it came an inner voice, "Speak! Speak to her in my name."

A battle raged within Paul. What should he say? Was this but his own feelings toward the girl? He wanted to comply with the urging but was fearful that it might not be the leading of the Spirit of God. The urge could not be denied. He could not hold back. He put down his work, arose, and stood over the girl, hands extended. He locked eyes with her. A strange light appeared to pass between them.

"Elana! Elana! Elana!" Three times he called her name. "Hear me!" he commanded. With this he gripped her hand, and she arose before him.

"In the name of Jesus of Nazareth, I command your mind to become aware. You shall become aware of those about you, aware of their feelings and needs. You shall become aware of your need for them. Even so be it."

For a moment everything was still. Paul watched her closely and perceived light dawning in her. Her face began to show life. Her eyes turned from one thing to another as if she were seeing them for the first time. Then she looked at her father and, with a small cry, ran toward him, threw her arms about his neck, and nestled her head on his shoulder.

Her father was overcome. Tears of joy flowed down his cheeks. He lifted up his eyes to the heavens and cried, "Glory to God. Jesus lives! He has this day come to my house through Paul."

Paul put his arm about them both as he led them to the door. "What wonders God does perform for those who believe. Remember always what God has done for you this day. The peace of God and the love of Jesus Christ go with you now and forever."

News of the healing of Elana spread through the city. Some marveled. Others scoffed. Daily there were crowds of people at his house. He could not carry on his trade because of the demands on his time. He prayed for the sick. He bore his testimony to all.

One night an angel came to Paul and said, "Get you up and return to Damascus, for the Lord has a great work for you to do. Tarry there a short time and then go to Jerusalem. Ere many months pass you will be called upon to enter into your work."

Paul departed the next day. Over two years had passed since that fateful event on the road to Damascus. What changes had been wrought in his life! Where once he had been a man of great power for hunting down those whom the Sanhedrin declared blasphemers, now he was the hunted and had to flee for his life. But he steadfastly went about his calling to preach the message of Jesus to the world.

Within his breast was a great longing to convert the Jews to their Messiah. Going to Jerusalem would afford him such a chance, he thought. Something of the old impatience still remained. Why could he not stay in the East? He was telling the message to many there. What he did not realize was that his return to Damascus was really the beginning of the spread of the gospel into the Roman world.

— — —

The walls of Damascus were thick. In order to move

soldiers quickly from one place to another in defense of the city, a narrow roadway had been built along the top. Small houses stood along the outer edge of the wall, their floor joists propped up by timbers for stability. Many of the inhabitants had built trapdoors into their floors so they could haul provisions up into the house without having to enter through the city gate. It was much easier just to let a rope down through the trap-door and pull the provisions up in a basket.

After arriving in Damascus Paul preached boldly in the synagogues, expounding the gospel of Jesus Christ. Many Jews took affront when they could not overcome his arguments. In desperation they enlisted the help of the Ethnarch and daily lay in ambush for the purpose of slaying him.

The elders realized it would be but a matter of time before the plot would be successful. They gathered to-gether in mighty prayer on his behalf. Finally, when it became apparent that the danger was too great, they persuaded Paul to leave the city and go to Jerusalem. They took him to a house on the wall. After dark, they had him stand with his feet in one of the large provision baskets to lower him to the ground outside. Hardly had they started to lower him than a squad of soldiers marched along the base of the wall, coming to a standstill almost below where Paul would be landing. They did not look up, but neither could Paul be lowered to the ground. His friends dared not haul him back up for fear that the creaking of the rope might betray them. So there they were, desperately hanging on to the rope while Paul hung halfway between the floor and the ground.

Ananias thought of a plan and quickly dispatched one of the youths to the gate where, after navigating the distance in record time, he shouted to the soldiers that a thief was escaping with a purse stolen from him. The soldiers responded quickly and searched along the street, without avail. While they were gone, Paul was lowered to the ground, and escaped the city in the darkness.

On the move again, Paul now made the journey to Jerusalem, following the same route he had traveled two years before.

This was no longer the man who had left the city with so much hatred in his heart. He had left his family in the home of his father and gone forth on a journey that had kept him from their side for nearly three years. He had gone forth with traditions engraved on his mind, learned in the ways taught by Gamaliel. He returned with an awesome love that included Jew and Gentile alike. The traditions were not lost but tested and refined in the crucible of the Spirit of God. Being a new man, he was no longer identified with the former Saul of Tarsus; he was truly Paul, the apostle. On many occasions he was to proclaim, "I have not been taught by the traditions of men, nor have I learned this gospel from them, but of Jesus Christ himself." He came back prepared for his apostleship, having spent the same amount of time at Jesus' feet as the other apostles who had walked the Palestinian roads with their Master.

Jerusalem was changed, too. The mark of the Nazarene was on that city. An unrest settled as a pall over the people. Already, the death of the city was beginning. The prediction of Jesus, "O Jerusalem . . . thy city is left unto thee desolate," was about to be realized—but only the spiritually aware sensed this. There was a steady exodus of Christians from the city. They dispersed throughout the whole Roman world.

Returning to his father's house, he found that he was bereft of family. His wife and two sons had been en route to the temple when a fracas broke out between the Jews and Romans. Helaman, leader of a band of zealots, had attacked a squad of soldiers who had taken one of their band into custody. The woman and her children were caught between the factions. No one knows exactly how it happened, but when the streets were cleared, among those who were dead upon the cobblestones were Paul's wife and the two sons. The grief over their deaths and the worry over his son was too much for Paul's father, and he had died a few months later.

Stricken, Paul went to the temple to pray. He knelt with his shawl pulled over his head in silent grief. His voice was raised in prayer, "Give ear, O Lord, to the words of my mouth. Hearken unto my cry. For I am desolate with grief. My soul is heavy. I know that you are not a God who takes pleasure in wickedness, but wickedness has slain my beloved." Thus he poured out his grief upon the altar of the Lord. His shoulders heaved with sobbing. Then there came a time of calm, a time of waiting. It was as if he were listening for a reply. And a voice came to him, saying, "My son, they are with me. Grieve not, for they are not lost. Go down into the city and find Peter and James. I shall prepare the way before you through Barnabas, for the work unto which I have called you is soon to begin."

Paul entered the gates of the temple, stood in his place and looked toward the heavens. His face was aglow with a heavenly light. Those about him knew something had happened but did not know what it was. They shrank back in awe as most people do in the presence of that which they do not understand. He turned and made his way through the court, past the gates of the temple, and into the city. Led by an inner guide, he walked toward the northern edge of the city.

His trip from Damascus had not been unannounced.

Barnabas, the Generous, had kept in touch. It had pleased him to know that Paul was a man with a mission. He had gone to tell Peter and James all that he had learned about his friend.

Peter and James had reservations about Paul. Too many of their friends had been victims of the persecution of the Jews for them to forget that Paul was one of their chief inquisitors. But Barnabas told them of the Damascus experience. He declared that the hand of the Lord had been laid upon Saul, the persecuter, changing him to Paul, the apostle, who defended the Christian cause in the synagogues. He told of how Paul had received ministry while in Arabia. He told of the power of healing that had been evidenced through him.

Peter was the first to become convinced. "Brethren," he said, "you will recall how it was with me in the city of Joppa when the Lord showed me the great sailcloth filled with creatures of the sea and bade me eat thereof. I call to your mind how this was in preparation for the coming of Cornelius, the Gentile centurian. You know that he was divinely led into our fellowship. If God can do such a thing—granting the power of his spirit to a man whose life had been dedicated to the pursuit of war—who are we to deny that he can also change a man such as this Paul? I am willing to allow him fellowship with us under the sponsorship of Barnabas."

And so it was that Barnabas went searching for Paul at the same time that Paul was leaving the temple. They met along the way, as if it had been prearranged, and the power of Christian love flowed once more between them. The contributer of his wealth to the poor took Paul by the hand and led him to the apostles.

Peter and James were the only apostles in the city at that time. They had many questions to ask, and Paul had many for them. They talked into the night of the next day. Each learned from the other, and the Spirit of God taught them all.

The next day Paul walked toward the temple, filled with a desire to share his expanded faith with his fellow Jews. But he had hardly gotten inside the gates before he was recognized and confronted by some members of the Sanhedrin.

"We have heard of your traitorous acts, Saul of Tarsus," said one—his voice filled with sarcasm.

Paul held up his hand to speak, but his words were drowned by a chorus of voices. Bedlam resulted as others joined in the confrontation. Soon there was an angry mob, and Paul fled the scene.

He returned another day. Word was out that there was to be no more demonstrations in the temple. The Roman governor had been informed of the near-riot, called the leaders before him, and informed them that a recurrence would make it necessary for him to station soldiers in the court.

Although Paul was allowed to kneel and pray, his soul was troubled. No overt effort was made against him, but he was well aware that the Jews had vowed to put him to death at the first opportune moment. The question of how effective his ministry in Jerusalem might be was uppermost in his mind.

As he prayed, an aura of light surrounded him. It was not a searing light, such as he had encountered on the Damascus road, but it was of the same Source. He lifted his eyes, and the whole temple melted from his view. Jesus was standing above him, saying, "Thou art my son whom I have rescued from the way of error. The Jews will not receive your testimony of me. Make haste and get out of Jerusalem. Go! I will send you far from here to the Gentiles."

This was the third time the Lord had stated that

Paul's mission was to be to the Gentiles.

The brethren, anxious for Paul's safety, escorted him to Caesarea Stratonis by the sea during the night. They placed him on a ship plying the coast to the north. He disembarked at his home city of Tarsus. Here he remained until, months later, Barnabas came for him to accompany him to Antioch of Syria. It was from the congregation there that the two disciples were commissioned to make their first missionary journey.

— — —

Paul had talked on and on into the night. We sat spellbound as he related event after event. The pink light of morning light was coloring the East when he ceased.

My heart pounded within me. My excitement grew until I felt that I would burst. Never had I heard such an incredible story. Yet, I doubted not a word of it. God had done astounding things with this man. Now he was working in me. Paul the Pharisee, a good man with strong religious ties, had moved out of the mediocrity of legalism into the extraordinary realm of Christian faith. As this man's life had been turned about, I felt that mine also was being changed in much the same way.

The amazing fact was that no human agency had intervened in the call, but at the same time human agency was used to crown the calling. If nothing more had happened on the road to Damascus than the blinding light and Saul's resultant loss of sight, the event would have been but a historical event to be forgotten or shrugged off as a result of too much sun or too much brooding over dark events. But the event did not stop there. God had intervened in the life of a specific man, at a definite time, and in a particular place. The intervention was strong and clear, but Saul was not left to grovel in the dust as a sorry sinner. Other lives were involved. A specific man was called to minister to him. It had never oc-

curred to me that such an act of God could ever occur—but it happened, and I was thrilled by it.

Porphia and I left the house and walked back toward
our abode. The chill of the night caused her to shiver. I
put my cloak around her shoulders and drew her close
to me as we walked, timing our steps so they coincided.
We were silent most of the way, each lost in thoughts of
the experiences of the day and evening.

Chapter 4

It was well into late summer when Paul announced he was ready to continue his journey. He had stayed according to my advice. Each Sabbath he taught in the synagogue. But controversy began early, and when the leaders saw that Paul was attracting a strong following they met in secret. The leader, Platonius, was chief rabbi, and his word was respected. He said, "This man speaks of Jesus, the Nazarene, as if he were God. No man who has been hanged upon a tree can be revered; he is accursed."

This accusation was relayed to me by a friend. When I went to Platonius to speak of the matter, he was cordial at first. As if teaching a small child, he repeated his accusation. "It is written: 'For he that is hanged is accursed of God.' So Jesus could not be the Anointed One. He was hanged."

"But," I argued, "that was done by the Romans. He was not hanged by the Jewish tribunal."

Platonius began to get red in the face, and the veins stood out along his neck. "Thou art a fool!" he proclaimed. "It was the people's judgment. And furthermore, it is the judgment of the elders of the synagogue that Paul is a blasphemer and a traitor to this people." He turned from me and spoke no more.

It became apparent that Platonius' ideas were bearing fruit in part of the congregation. Most of the leaders were very cool toward Paul. Some began to pick at anything he said, seeking to find fault.

At last it came to a head. On a Sabbath, having placed the tallith upon my head and covering my shoulders with my shawl, I entered the synagogue and took my usual place. Platonius recited the prayers, reading them in the language of the city. The law was read in Hebrew, the sacred scroll having been handed from the Ark and placed before the reader. The Prophets were read next. It was time for the commentary. Paul arose to speak, but Platonius deliberately snubbed him and called upon another elder. The snub did not go unnoticed. A ripple ran through the congregation. A murmur began and swelled until someone shouted, "Let Paul speak!" Other voices were raised. The leaders sought in vain to silence them.

Paul saw that there would be a riot if he did nothing. Standing, with his favorite gesture, he silenced the congregation. Then he spoke: "Men and brethren, I would have you remember that we are worshipers of the true God. Let us not have these riotings. I will retire from this place. It is fitting that I do so. But let it be known that I first brought this message to the Jews. As so often happens, when their congregation is swelled with Gentiles, the Jews feel threatened. I shall go, and I shall take the message to the Gentiles."

With these words, Paul turned from the sanctuary and left the building. Over half of the congregation left with him and followed him to a spot outside the city where he sat down. There they gathered around him, and he taught them.

The rift did not heal, however. It grew. Some of the women of the congregation incited actions against Paul wherever he sought to meet. Under this cloud, he appointed elders to care for the work; then he and Barnabas left the city and headed eastward toward the city of Iconium.

I remained behind. My duties demanded that I do so, but I did not return to the synagogue. I was disillusioned by the manner in which the leaders had treated the followers of Paul. Their argument were about such petty and artificial matters that the central message was lost entirely. They were closed to reason. In turn, I was separated from them because I was a friend of Paul. I went about my work as a physician.

A different relationship had developed between Porphia and me. Our experiences with Paul had brought us another dimension of common concern. Now, a third dimension entered in. No longer was she my aide; I saw her as a desirable woman. When our hands touched as we worked with a patient, I found my heartbeat quickening. When she looked up at me, I wanted to press my lips to hers.

One afternoon we were cleaning up the reception room after all of my patients were gone. It was hot and sticky. I suggested that we go to the roof and rest in the shade of the great tree that grew next to the western edge of the house.

"You go," she urged. "I shall come soon."

Wearily I climbed the steps and unrolled a mat in the shade. Lying back upon it, I felt a cool breeze moving through the tree with the soft sound of a maiden humming to herself. I was relaxing when Porphia came. She had changed from her coarse work dress into a soft garment that was fastened about the waist with a cord. In her hands she carried a tray. Upon it was a piece of cheese and a bottle of wine.

I moved over on the mat, and she knelt down beside me, placing the tray upon the floor. "You are very tired. I thought you would like food and drink."

Our eyes met and held. Then she looked down— demurely. At that moment she became the most desirable woman in all the world to me.

That day we sought the elders to consecrate our union—we became husband and wife.

Chapter 5

Porphia and I worked diligently together in our new-found happiness. Between caring for patients during the day and meeting with the congregation at night, we had little time for anything else. Twice I had been asked to go to nearby communities to tell of our faith.

Late one summer night we were awakened by a knock at the door. Porphia was going to answer, but I was already out of bed and went to the window to see who it was.

A youth stood at the door. His dark hair was plastered with perspiration against his forehead.

"What do you want?" I called down to him.

"Is this the home of Luke, the physician?" he asked.

I could not see his face clearly, but the light of the moon fell on him when he stepped out of the shadows. It was then that I saw his heaving breast. He apparently had been running.

"I am Luke," I replied, waiting for an answer to my question.

"I come from Paul. He needs you." There was a tone of desperation in his voice.

"I will be right down," I called.

Girding my robe, I went quickly down the stairs. Porphia followed me. I opened the door and let him in, then latched it securely. Since becoming Christians, we were troubled by the Jews who caused considerable mischief by harassing us and threatening to do us harm. Only the fact that I was well known and liked by the rest of the community kept them from overt actions. I took no chances and was careful for our safety at all times.

We moved into the reception room. Here I lighted the

lamp so I could see my visitor more clearly. He appeared to be about eighteen—somewhat taller than I, but of slight build. His hair lay in wet ringlets about his forehead, and his face was flushed from exertion. His legs and feet were dirty from the dust of the road.

Turning to me, he cried, "They stoned him! The priests of Jupiter and the Jews stoned him!"

He collapsed on the floor and rocked back and forth. "A-a-ii! A-a-ii," he wailed.

I knelt down beside him and put my arms about his shoulders. Almost fearfully I asked, "Is he alive?"

"Yes," he replied, "just barely. He sent me for you."

"Where is he?" I asked.

"In Lystra, at the home of my mother."

I thought for a moment. Lystra was east of Iconium. It would take two days of hard travel to get there. By now, Porphia had come into the room carrying a basin and towel. I had the youth sit up while she washed his feet and legs. Then drawing a box of ointment from beneath her skirt, she salved the stone bruises and cuts she had uncovered.

We continued our conversation. "Who are you?" I asked.

"I am sorry," he said, "I should have told you. I am Timothy, son of Joash. My father is dead. My mother, Eunice, cares for me."

When Porphia had finished she said, "I shall go and prepare food."

"Prepare food and clothing for a journey," I called to her. "I must go to Paul. He is hurt."

"I heard," she replied in her staid manner.

Turning to Timothy I said, "Tell me what happened."

By now the lad had gotten control of himself, but at first his words made little sense. He jumped from thing to thing, event to event, without any chronology. Finally I stopped him and suggested, "Why don't you tell me the story from the beginning?"

He paused to regroup his thoughts, and began again.

When Paul and Barnabas had left Antioch, they took the well-traveled road toward Iconium. The trip was too long to make in a single day. Paul, in his weakened condition, was unable to travel as fast as usual, so they stopped at a wayside inn on the evening of the next day. Late in the night a band of brigands trooped into the inn and began to loot the place. Barnabas was the first to awaken. He shook Paul to rouse him, but before they could make their escape, two of the band burst into their room and demanded their valuables. Finding that they carried little with them, the bandits began to beat them with staves and threw their meager furnishings about, inflicting painful injuries on both Barnabas and Paul.

When the bandits were gone, it was discovered that they had murdered the innkeeper. Some of the men were more seriously injured than Paul or Barnabas. Two of the women had been brutally ravished. While Paul sought to help the guests and make them as comfortable as possible, the sound of chariots was heard. A Roman centurion and his company drew up at the inn and, when apprised of what had happened, he sent part of his men out to pursue the bandits and stationed others about the inn.

The death of the innkeeper was considered a serious matter, for he had provided a relief station to the soldiers. The caravan was delayed a full day while the matter was investigated. Toward midday the searchers returned with four prisoners. Barnabas recognized two as those who had broken into their room. One of the women identified another. The fourth was not recognized, but the centurion kept him prisoner because he had been found in company with the others. He questioned them with the whip and afterward bound them in chains and took them with him. A squad of soldiers were left to escort the travelers to Iconium lest there be some of the band lingering about.

When Barnabas and Paul arrived in Iconium they sought out friends who had been recommended by followers at Antioch. They were given a room in the home of Epaphras, a cousin of Achaicus.

On the Sabbath they made their way to the synagogue. The congregation listened to Paul as he told of the coming of the Anointed One. Weeks passed, and many who flocked about these men to listen and learn were converted.

Word of their success got back to Antioch. Platonius was furious. He wrote an epistle to the leader of the Iconium synagogue and sent it by messenger. Accompanying the messenger were some busybodies who had been influenced by Platonius' accusations. Their arrival at the synagogue stirred up considerable controversy. In the epistle Paul was accused of blasphemy and labeled a traitor to the Jews of Jerusalem. The hangers-on swore that he had taught a corrupt religion. Among them were some disgruntled members who proclaimed that Paul was not presenting the pure teachings of Jesus but a doctrine of his own. They attracted leaders of the synagogue, who felt their position was being threatened by the popularity of the two missionaries.

Notwithstanding this, a large congregation of believers remained faithful to the teachings and, in order to remove the irritation felt within the synagogue, they withdrew and met in another part of the city.

Iconium, one of the more ancient settlements of Galatia, was the home of a proud and prosperous people. But, being a free city, there was no strong Roman authority present. Thus it was that the opposing Jews and some of the other dissidents were able to stir up enough trouble to come to the attention of the city fathers. Paul and Barnabas were taken into custody, questioned, and released. But a conspiracy developed that threatened to lead to their being dragged out of the city for stoning. When Barnabas told Paul what was happening, they met with the elders of the congregation who deemed it wise for them to head south by west, then turn toward Lystra, located at the foot of Black Mountain.

Lystra was not a city that Paul might have chosen under other circumstances. Though there was no established Jewish community, some Jews were present. This led the travelers to the home of Eunice, a Jewess who had married a Gentile. To them had been born a son Timothy, who—after his father's death—was reared according to the traditions of the Jews.

Early in their stay in Lystra, Paul was preaching at the gate of the city. Among those assembled was a cripple whose whole being was caught up with the message. His face, aglow with his faith, caught the apostle's eye. Paul sensed the aura that often came over him when the spirit of discernment directed him to minister to specific individuals. Turning to the man, he commanded, "Stand upright on your feet!" Reminiscent of the healing in Jerusalem near the golden gate of the temple, when Peter and John had brought the blessing of healing to a beggar, it seemed as if the event were being repeated when the man leaped up and began to walk.

This had an electrifying effect on those assembled. The miraculous healing before their eyes called to mind a long-held tradition that had been encouraged by the priests of the temple of Jupiter. The reaction was immediate. Citizens ran to the pagan priest and rehearsed the event to him with embellishments. Donning his most ornate robes, the priest hurried to the site. Fixing his eyes upon Paul and Barnabas, he sonorously proclaimed:

"Behold, my people, Jupiter has chosen us for a visit," pointing toward Barnabas, who stood head and shoulders above the crowd. Then, pointing to Paul he continued, "And Mercury, his spokesman, accompanies him. I know them well, for they have visited me in the temple often."

Trying to glean as much as possible from the event, he ordered that an ox be brought and an altar erected that a fitting sacrifice be offered on the spot of the healing.

When it became apparent to Paul what was happening, he was very distressed. He sought to stop the preparations, but the turmoil was so great he had difficulty in getting the people's attention. At last, by climbing upon the pile of faggots that were stacked for the sacrifice, and raising his hand, he quieted them enough that his voice could be heard.

"Please cease these preparations! We are men like you. We have come to teach you to turn from the ways of idolatry and to worship the only true God. He has left witness of his being, and have shown you his power."

This embarrassed the priest of Jupiter before his followers. Many felt that they had been tricked by the newcomers in the city. They had been set for a celebration, and now they felt cheated.

Paul returned to the home of Eunice. Timothy, who had been attracted to the apostle from the beginning, found that the day's events raised many questions in his mind.

Not all of the populace turned away from Paul. Many thoughtful people had come to hear what this strange man had to say. After hearing, they remained to believe and to find their lives enriched.

The mischief-makers, however, did not remain idle. When they heard that Paul was in Lystra, they followed. To their number had been added some who believed part of the message but clung to the Jewish rites. They considered the Christian doctrine an extension of Judaism; it was all right to accept the teachings of Jesus as long as one also kept the Jewish traditions. Everywhere Paul appeared, they stirred trouble.

On a dark, rainy night in late summer Paul and Barnabas were making their way back to their abode. Timothy was with them. Deeply involved in a discussion of the nature of the resurrection, Timothy turned to ask a question only to discover that Paul was not beside him. He called and received no answer. Barnabas, who had been a few steps in front of them, ran back to an alley where he found Paul's tunic. Alarmed, they searched all around but saw nothing more. Coming out on the far end, they found a crowd gathering. Suddenly it dawned upon them where Paul was. He had been spirited from them by his enemies who now were stoning him. Barnabas was in the midst of the crowd in a matter of seconds, His big arms swinging this way and that, sending bodies back against the buildings as if they were pieces of firewood. Timothy joined him. The noise attracted the soldiers on patrol and, as they approached, the persecutors fled.

Paul lay as if dead on the cobblestones. However, when Barnabas leaned over his companion he discovered there was breath still in him. Gently he carried his wounded friend to the home of Eunice. By morning, Paul was burning with fever. Though they salved his wounds and bathed his burning brow, he did not seem to respond. A local physician came but shook his head after examining the battered body. He gave them no hope for survival.

It was then that Timothy was dispatched to fetch me.

"I hope he still lives," Timothy cried as we hurried along the way.

Sadly I lifted my thoughts in prayer to God. "Oh Lord, you have sent my friend Paul on this journey. Surely you will not let the enemy prevail. Go before me and preserve him, and I will do all within my power to help."

The next afternoon we arrived in Iconium but did not pause there. Early the next morning we reached Lystra. Tired and dusty from our journey, we were met at the door by Barnabas. Standing behind him was Eunice, who hurried to bring us basins of water.

As soon as I was washed I went to Paul. Pale and wan he lay on the pallet. His eyes were closed, but when I entered, they opened, and he weakly raised his hand. "Luke, my friend. Thank God you have come."

"I came as quickly as I could," I said, taking his hand in mine. And even as I touched his burning flesh, I felt communion between us.

I examined him carefully. The bruises were bad in places and should have been lanced, but too much time had passed; the blood already had solidified. Time would take care of that. His scalp had been cut in several places, and I feared there might be a concussion that might incapacitate him for a long time. There was a broken bone in one arm. I set that and put splints on to hold it in place. Infection appeared in some of the cuts, and I used an unguent to take away the redness. I spent most of the evening treating his wounds, then gave him some herbs to ease his pain. He fell asleep shortly thereafter. Barnabas stayed beside him, while Timothy and I retired. I left instructions for Barnabas to call me if Paul became restless.

Paul rested well, and by morning his fever had abated. It appeared that he would recover. Prayers were offered on his behalf, and Barnabas anointed his head with oil. The miracle of God's healing power began to work. By the following day, Paul was moving about the room, and the next day he informed us that he was going to Derbe. We tried to dissuade him, but he was adamant. When I offered to go with him he insisted that I return to Antioch.

"You are needed in Antioch," he urged, "and I am going to be all right. I will come through Antioch when I start my journey back to Jerusalem."

Thus it was that we bade one another farewell. When I arrived home the morning of the second day, Porphia greeted me warmly. She had been kept busy with my patients and had referred some to my colleague, Marconius. But I was pleased with her work. She had learned much while assisting me and seldom made a mistake. More than that, I was pleased to be with her again.

The winter months had come and gone. Spring flowers were blooming. Porphia had added the woman's touch to our upper room and had potted plants setting on the ledges of the rooftop. Our life was rich with the fellowship of the church in the city. Something wonderful had happened to our lives since Paul had brought us into the fellowship. Porphia never looked more desirable. Much of her stoicism had been shed, and she carried herself with assurance.

We were dining after a busy day when she looked across to me.

"I have something to say," she offered. There was a shyness in her manner yet a twinkle in her eyes.

"Speak up," I said, with mock sternness.

"I am with child," she announced.

With a cry of happiness I arose, picked her up in my arms, and held her close to me.

"You shall present me with a beautiful child," I said.

She snuggled against me, and our happiness was full. Then there was a knock at our door. Impatient with the interruption in this very special moment, I threw back the shutter and looked down. It was Paul and Barnabas.

"Open up, my friend," cried Paul. "We have come to tarry with you as we head for Jerusalem."

I turned to Porphia, but she had already heard and was on the way down the steps to let them in. We were glad to see them, and as they sat and ate of the repast we furnished they brought us up to date on the progress of the church in Galatia.

They had found a good reception in Derbe and remained there several months. It has been their intent to go from there to Tarsus so they could visit the churches in Cilicia where Paul had ministered before Barnabas had called him to Antioch of Syria. But the early winter snows had closed the passes, so they returned to Lystra to find that the furor against them had died down. They were able to preach without the dangers that had attended their earlier time in the city.

From there they went to Iconium, where their experience was the same. In each place the church flourished, and missionaries were being sent out into the surrounding cities with good success. By the time Paul and Barnabas had ministered in these cities winter was over, and they arrived at our doorstep in early spring.

I reported that the church in Antioch was showing promise of becoming a hub from which the work could grow. Our congregations were increasing in number and size daily.

Our friends remained with us just long enough to meet with the members in Antioch. Here they were received with much affection, and Paul's message was one of encouragement.

Before the week was over, they began their journey back to Jerusalem, agreeing not to tarry in the lowland. The fact that there was to be a conference in Jerusalem made haste necessary. We bade them farewell after praying for their safety. As they departed, we walked to the edge of the city with them. Our hearts went with them, but we knew our work was here.

Chapter 6

The time of the Passover was nigh. We were preparing to celebrate the resurrection of our Lord when a messenger arrived with an epistle from Paul.

Paul, a servant of God and an apostle of Jesus Christ, unto Luke, my fellow workman in the faith. The Grace of God be with you in all you do. I recall the good spirit that was born within you and Porphia at Antioch and the times when you ministered unto me in my times of need.

Much has happened since we were with you. The church at Jerusalem is growing in strength and to the glory of God.

Barnabas and I have parted. He will take John Mark with him to Cyprus where he will visit the congregations we established there. I intend to take the northern route through Cilicia, coming into Galatia from the mountains to the east. The Judaisers have done much mischief among the congregations there and I would visit them and strengthen them. I may send them an epistle since I cannot get there before the summer months.

I intend to visit Antioch after Iconium. From there I would go into Bithynia to tell the story there and to plant the seed of the good news in the hearts of as many as the Lord may allow.

I am writing you to ask that you prepare yourself to go with me when I leave Antioch. My affliction still plagues me and I would call upon you to keep me strong and able.

Give my greetings to Porphia and to the congregation in your city. I will look forward to seeing you when I arrive and pray that you will see fit to travel with me for a while.

I read and reread the message. I really wanted to do all I could in the work, but for me to leave my home to go with Paul had not entered my mind. I shared this with Porphia, and we talked long into the night about the request. We now had an infant son, so Porphia could not travel with me. I felt I had a duty to remain at home and care for them.

At first Porphia was very quiet as she gave thought to what we had received. She arose, went to the cradle, and picked up the little one, cuddling him in her arms. Opening her dress, she began to nurse him. We sat there silently, each thinking. Finally, I spoke.

"I am not strong enough to make this decision alone. Let us pray to our God. If this is to be, we will come to know. If it is not, we will know, too."

She looked up at me, her face sober. Her eyes held the sign of love within them. "If it is God's will, he will take care of us," she said.

The next days were strange ones. We continued to care for the sick during the day and to meet nightly with the congregation, but our inner peace was disturbed. For the first time we felt our lives together being threatened. I could not conceive of God willing that I should abandon my family. At the same time, I felt an urge to go with Paul to expand the work into new places. Porphia and I talked and prayed together for light. The light came in a strange way.

We were worshiping with a small group of the faithful on a warm and sultry night. The stars were hidden behind a curtain of clouds. Occasionally the moon would show through the translucent curtains and, as if frightened, would recede again. No breeze was blowing, but a sound could be heard high in the air—as sometimes happens when the winds are on their way to earth from heaven. There was an uneasiness among us that could not be stilled. Each person present was anxious to be at home before the winds came.

Our meeting was interrupted by the sound of heavy footsteps outside, then a loud pounding on our host's door. When he opened it, there stood two stalwart Roman soldiers. Over their shoulders we could see the face of a man in a helmet.

"We were told that Luke the physician was at this place," one of the soldiers stated. There was no attempt to enter the building. But when a Roman soldiers calls in the night, it always bodes ill for someone.

Porphia gripped my arm in fear. I stepped forward and said, "I am Luke. I am a physician."

When I had identified myself, the soldier in the helmet pushed the two soldiers in front of him aside. By his attire I recognized him of the rank of centurion. His shoulders filled the doorway, blocking our view of those behind him. His face was stern but not threatening. He spoke, "I am Melchius of Caesar's army. I come on a mission of mercy. May I enter?"

Our host nodded, and I stepped back. As he entered, he removed his helmet from his head. His hair was as black as the night. Though he remained standing, he relaxed somewhat, and we were all put at ease. His soldiers remained outside the house.

He continued, "I have charge of the escort of an important prisoner. We are en route to Ephesus where we will engage passage to Rome. This afternoon the prisoner was seized by a demon and has caused much trouble to us and to himself. Because he has been a man of importance, I am reluctant to restrain him with chains all of the way."

He paused for a moment to choose his words carefully. "I have been told that you can provide potions that will calm him and keep him under control."

"I will have to see the man before I can know whether or not it is possible," I said.

"By Jupiter!" he cried. "If you can help it will be much easier for my prisoner." He paused for a moment and added, "And for me as well."

"Take the prisoner to my house," I said. "I will show you the way."

Turning to Porphia, I bade her get the child and come with me. We left the meeting and led the way to our home. Opening the door and lighting lamps, we ushered the centurion in. Following him were four soldiers who escorted the prisoner.

I looked at this man who was in custody. He was tall, slender, and dressed in regal garb. His face wore the expression of one haunted by many woes. Even as he was brought into the room, he began to struggle with his captors.

"I don't want to go," he cried. "Don't make me go." He fell on the floor and began to writhe as if in great pain.

I had them bring him to a table, place him on it, and hold him so I could begin my examination.

"This is not like him," the centurion offered. "All the way from Jerusalem he has been docile and cooperative."

"You say this attack came on this afternoon?" I queried.

"Yes."

"Has he had any other attacks before?"

"No."

There was no fever. His heart was beating wildly, and his breathing was rapid. This could be caused by the emotional stress of being afraid. The fear had been building within him for days as they made their way along the roads.

I prepared a draught of herbs and started to hand it to the man. He shrank from me. "No! No! You are trying to poison me," he cried.

I sat the beaker down and turned from him, saying, "All right. You do not have to take it." I went about cleaning up where I had prepared the mixture.

He watched me carefully. The soldiers looked to their leader who nodded to indicate that they were to continue to hold the man. The patient was shaking as if he were cold. I continued to ignore him.

After a few minutes he calmed down. "What's in it?" he asked.

"Something to help you relax," I replied.

"A drink of wine would be better," he ventured.

"No it wouldn't," I countered. "Wine can disguise many things. You are afraid you will be poisoned. If I were to try to poison you, I would use wine, but I have none."

He seemed to think that over. I could see when he had made up his mind, for his shoulders raised and dropped as he heaved a sigh. "Give it to me," he said. I handed it to him, and he drank it in one gulp.

Later, when the draught had taken effect, I had the soldiers step back so I could talk to the man.

"Why are you so afraid?" I asked.

"I have enemies," he replied, and as he spoke his eyes searched the room as if they might be lurking behind the furnishings.

"Can you tell me about them?" I pressed.

For a moment I thought he was going to refuse, but again he sighed and began to talk. He told of having been a ruler in Jerusalem, a representative of Caesar. He talked of how intrigue and political maneuvering made his rule so hard.

"The Jews," he said, "are a most difficult people to rule. They live by their own laws and make their own rules. But I ruled them fairly, and they respected me for it. I interpreted the law in their favor often." He paused as if thinking, then continued, "And that is where I made a mistake."

"How is that?" I queried.

"Ah, that is where I made a mistake," he repeated, as if I had not spoken. "From the day they brought one of their own people before me and accused him of being a traitor to Caesar, I have found no peace. Everything has gone wrong. Nothing I have tried has been successful. Oh, I bent the law a little to let them have their way. We crucified their prisoner on the hill of the skull."

He paused again as if reliving some of those days. Then, when I thought he was through, he continued. "You know, they told me later that he was raised from the dead. Can you imagine that? Raised from the dead!" His laughter echoed through the room. All of us were quiet as this deranged man spoke of his life. Then he leaned forward and in a conspiratorial tone said, "From that day to this everything has gone wrong. And I can't even remember his name."

"What is your name?" I asked.

"Do you not know? I am Pilate." With these words, he laid back on the table and went to sleep. The potion had worked well.

I turned to the centurion. "If you will bring a litter, you can take him. I don't believe he will cause you any more trouble." I turned to the table behind me and picked up a small pouch. "If he should have another attack, mix this with water and give it to him."

The officer thanked me. As he drew two gold pieces from his girdle he pressed them in my hand, saying, "Take this for your trouble."

"Why is he under arrest?" I asked.

"He was one of the group who sought to assassinate Caesar," he replied.

After they had left the room, the import of what had happened began to dawn on me. I had met the man who had sentenced Jesus. And now he was being taken to Rome for the same type of crime as he had sentenced Jesus for. What a price he was paying for his willingness to compromise his principles.

Porphia moved to my side. Tears were running down

her cheeks She sensed the same thing I had.

"I should hate him," she said sadly, "but I feel only pity. His decision led to the crucifixion of the Son of God."

"Yes," I said, "and his plight has answered our prayers. We must never compromise when God opens up ways for us to serve him. When Paul comes, I must go with him."

Chapter 7

A year had passed since we had bade Paul farewell as he began his return journey to Jerusalem. Six months ago we had received his epistle and then came face to face with Pilate. Porphia and I made careful plans for me to be ready when Paul arrived. Marconius had been joined by a young apprentice who showed great promise as a physician. They agreed to care for my patients during my absence. Achaicus offered to watch over Porphia, and Julia would stay with her. Other members of the congregation pledged to see that she did not want, though I felt I had enough permanent income to take care of her.

"You will need a heavy coat," Porphia said to me one day. "The weather gets very cold in Bithynia." With this she brought out a woolen coat that she had sewn with her own hands. I slid it around my shoulders. The fit was perfect.

"Your thoughtfulness amazes me," I exclaimed. "You are always looking out for my comfort and well-being."

"I do no more than you do for me," she countered as I drew her close.

Every day was filled with thoughts of preparation. It was well into the summer when we saw Paul and his companion making their way down the long street that led to our house. As they trudged toward us I could tell that Paul was faltering. Before I could move, Porphia ran to his side, and her strong arms went about him to bear him up. Thus he was escorted into the house.

"Luke, my friend, how glad I am to see you," Paul cried. "You can tell that it has been a hard journey. I am tired and need a night of rest before we are on our way." With that he sank on the pallet in exhaustion.

I knelt beside him. "Paul, you are always welcome in our house. Your presence brings light and joy within its walls." Our hands met and squeezed in silent communication.

Paul turned on his side and beckoned the youth who had accompanied him to his side. "This is Silas," he said. "You will find him a worthy friend and fellow traveler. The Spirit of God burns brightly in him."

Before me stood a youth of about nineteen summers. He was short and stocky, much like Paul. His arms and legs showed muscular development that spoke of great strength. His face was round and open; he seemed to be a person to be trusted. We embraced. When his arms went about me I was crushed against him. He was a very strong man—the kind who would be a good companion for Paul. I missed Barnabas, but this young disciple held promise of becoming equally as dear to me.

Porphia came into the room with a tray of wine, cheese, bread, and dates and set it before our guests. As they ate I watched Paul carefully, observing him as my patient. His skin was weathered by the sun and wind, but it bore a transparency that spoke of ill health. When he took food, he swallowed hard. The bags under his eyes were heavy. Only his inner resolve kept him going.

"Did you receive my letter?" he asked, looking up at me.

I was not prepared for his question, because I was deep in thought about his physical condition. Jerked back to the present I fumbled for words. "Yes! It came last winter." I changed the subject. "We have a child now."

"Oh, may I see it?" he asked.

Porphia, her face aglow with pride, brought the baby to him and placed him in his arms. Paul looked long upon him as he smiled into his face. A pudgy fist reached up and grasped Paul's nose. We burst into laughter as he struggled to loosen the little one's grasp.

"Now, that is my nose, and I am stuck with it. You cannot have it as a toy." Paul became a different person with a child in his arms. Some of the intensity drained from him; he became relaxed and at ease. I could see that he loved children.

"What is your name, my little friend?" Paul asked.

Porphia spoke up quickly. "He is Lucian, named after his father."

"Ah, Lucian. That is a good name," said Paul. Lifting up his eyes to the heavens, he solemnly proclaimed, "Oh, God, thou who dost know our end as well as our beginning, I present this child of Luke and Porphia whose name is Lucian, unto thee. May thy blessings rest upon him, and may the knowledge of Jesus Christ be instilled in his heart, that he may be a gracious and strong servant of thine unto the world." So saying, he handed the child back to its mother.

"Porphia," he continued, "I charge you with Lucian's care, for I discern that he will be a force for good in his maturity. Though you may carry much of the burden of his rearing, the Comforter will be with you and aid you in times of need."

Turning to me, Paul said, "Luke, you are a servant of the most high God. Soon you will embark on a great task in his name. But the Spirit will be with you and return you to your family that your lives together will be blessed."

I was nonplussed. Though I had not given my friend my answer he was acting as if I would go with him. Maybe I read too much in what he said to us, but I felt that he had foreknowledge of my acceptance. I believe Paul sensed my feelings and, to save me from embarrassment, he put his hand upon my shoulder and said,

"You are going to accompany me, are you not?"

I nodded my head. "Porphia and I have made the decision together. All is arranged for me to go whenever you are ready."

I looked at him sternly. "Paul, you are in no condition to make the journey right now. As your physician, I recommend several days of rest."

There was a stiffening of his back. A driven man, he was not an easy patient to treat. There were never enough hours in the day to get all done that he wanted to do. While traveling, he doggedly pressed on to his goal as if reluctant to stop, lest the goal not be there when he arrived. And even when he stopped, he always seemed to find someone with whom to talk, sharing the gospel into the night so that he got few hours of sleep.

Paul never seemed to meet a stranger. This went well with his personality. He never liked to build upon another's foundation, and even was reluctant to build upon his own. He was always pushing toward new frontiers. But the toll was great on his physical resources. I was insistent that he regain his strength before starting the long, hard journey northward to Bithynia. The terrain was mountainous, and the best roads were often washed away by flash floods. Bandits hid among the rocks to prey upon the unwary. Only the hearty should try such a trip.

I thought for a moment that Paul was going to refuse to stay, but though he was determined to get there as soon as possible, he was not a foolish man. My determination must have convinced him that I was not demanding something unreasonable.

"Very well," he said after a moment. "I have asked you to be my physician, and it behooves me to listen to your advice. But," he added, "do not be too cautious, lest we find ourselves traveling during the latter rains."

For three days he rested. I am not certain it was the kind of rest I would have preferred, for every day there was almost a constant stream of people coming to my door and wanting to talk to him. Paul thrived on this. But at least we were not engaged in strenuous physical exertion, and he could lie on his pallet as he talked.

One evening, when all had departed, we were talking about how it was that he found so much opposition in the work.

"I would think that anyone with an open mind could see that the way of Jesus Christ is the best way to live," I stated pompously.

"No matter where I go, Luke," he replied, "I always find people with a basic yearning for the truth. But among them there seems to be some who, for reasons of their own, do not want things to change. In fact, something within all of us resists change. If it were not so, the world would be in chaos all the time. No one could make decisions, for the basis of decision might change before implementation. God wants the very best there is in us, and that is what this gospel does; it challenges us to be our best."

"In the face of opposition," I added, "we still find many who cling to the message, once they have understood it."

"Yes, that basic yearning for goodness is stronger in some than in others. But remember that it is in all people. It is just harder to find in some than others." Paul's face shone with his earnestness.

"I am beginning to see something else," I said thoughtfully. "There must be opposition in all things. If it were not so, the truth would be hard to distinguish from mediocrity."

"Ah, it is written: 'I will hedge up thy way with thorns.' I can testify to that in my own life. Any time I turn aside from the purpose to which God has called me, opposition—like a wall of thorns—drives me back toward my calling," Paul mused. "But that very opposition has opened up ways for me to tell the story to more people. Because of it I am driven from one place to another. And I must ever be alert to the innate leadership ability among those I leave behind. Then, when I go, I find another place to work—and a new congregation is born."

At last the day arrived when we were to take our leave. We joined a small caravan awaiting us at the edge of the city and headed toward Mysia.

Porphia walked along with me for a little way, then bade me farewell with a lingering kiss. Our hands clung together until the very last, and as we walked over the hill, I turned back to see her standing there. She waved, and I raised my hand. Then we were out of sight.

We had one animal between the three of us to carry our belongings. Two of us walked beside him while one led. About midmorning we entered a canyon and stopped when the sun was at its zenith. After resting beneath some trees and cooling our feet in a stream, we were urged on by the caravan leader for he wanted to get to Mysia before nightfall.

Shortly after we had started again, we could see heavy clouds rolling over the rim of the mountains far ahead. Occasional lightning flashed but the rumble of thunder was slow in coming, so we knew the storm was distant.

Our leader seemed worried. Finally he fell back and said, "This is a dangerous area. Sudden floods have caught many travelers unaware, and they were never found. I want you to be prepared, and if I call you to climb to higher ground, do not pause for anything—not even your belongings."

The ominous news made us anxious, and we quickened our steps so we could get out of the canyon as soon as possible. We strode along without speaking, each caught up in his thoughts.

As we walked, I heard a new sound. At first it was as a rushing wind. The leader turned and shouted, "Everyone to high ground! A flood is on its way!"

There was much scurrying as we chose pathways to high places on the side of the canyon. Silas was leading our animal and tried to get it to climb with him.

"Silas!" I called. "Let him go and climb fast. He will take care of himself."

Hardly had the words come from my mouth before we saw a wall of water racing down the canyon, taking small trees and boulders with it. Paul was climbing ahead of me. Silas came up behind me, passed me, grabbed Paul's hand and drew him with him. We found a ledge beyond which we could not go, so we turned to see whether or not we were safe.

The water arrived where we had stood just moments before. One of the merchants who would not leave his laden animals was swept away in the tumultuous stream, his animals with him. The last we saw of them they were being buffeted by the waves and carried around a bend. Our little animal had found a spot where the waters just lapped at his legs.

We sat on our miserable perch, watching the flood go by. Slowly it began to subside, but it was late afternoon before we dared to go back down to the bottom. The mud was ankle-deep everywhere, and in some spots there were deep pockets that would swallow us. We searched about to find the other travelers. Finally, we had found everyone except the merchant. We were thankful that our caravan leader was wise enough to assess the dangers rightly.

It was too late for us to reach Mysia. The canyon was

too treacherous for us to try traveling in the dark. A council was held. Our leader suggested that we try to find a place where we could all stay together. After some searching, we found a ledge high on the side of the canyon with a small cave at one side. We dragged our belongings up to it, and tied the animals to trees. By pooling our belongings, we were able to make up a few beds in the cave where the three women and their companions could sleep. Ill equipped though we were, we found a heavy sword among us and used it to split wood. This we dried inside until we could use it to kindle a fire. Uncomfortable as we were Paul reminded us of the grace of God that had spared us and, if it had not been for his greed, the missing merchant might have been with us as well. Before we had settled down for rest, Paul gathered us about him and offered a prayer of thanksgiving for our good fortune to be alive. Before morning, sore from the uneven ground that seemed to poke into every part of my flesh, I had some doubts as to how fortunate we were.

With the sun came strong breezes that soon dried the ground beneath our feet. Our supply of food was sparse, but we all had enough to revive us. Shortly afterward, we were on our way through the canyon, headed toward Mysia. Our travel was slow, but we arrived at the gates of the city when the sun was high in the sky.

We took lodging at an inn, and after we had rested for a full day we sought out friends of Porphia. Through them, we were able to find a home where we could lodge while in the city. These friends were anxious to hear about her and rejoiced at the knowledge that she had borne a son. It took some explaining as to why she did not travel with me, but when they thought of the flood we had experienced, they agreed that such journeys were not for mothers and small babies.

Chapter 8

We rested until the evening of the Sabbath. After carefully preparing ourselves, we made our way to the synagogue and joined the men who were already assembled there. The women were at home with the children. After the worship, the men would return to their homes to continue the celebration of Sabbath with their families.

Tychicus, the reader for the congregation, was well versed in the scriptures. Paul was asked to speak, and Tychicus was fascinated with his interpretations—especially those concerning the expectations of the Jews having been fulfilled in Jesus Christ. At the close of the service he invited us to his home for a meal. We accepted.

When we arrived at the house, a short distance from the synagogue, Tychicus' daughter came running and drew him aside. After conferring for a few moments, he sent her away and turned toward us.

"Brethren," he said apologetically, "my daughter tells me that my wife has taken ill. This is not the hospitality I had expected to extend to you."

We stood there a moment; then Paul spoke, "Why not let Luke see her?"

Tychicus brightened, "Ah, yes. Perhaps a physician is what we need. We are fortunate that you have come to our home at this time."

I hesitated, yet felt it wise to offer my help. Before I could speak, Tychicus turned to me and asked, "Will you consent to see her?"

I am sure he had seen my hesitancy. I responded, "Certainly. Lead the way."

We entered, and the daughter took us to the room

where her mother lay. The wife of Tychicus was a comely woman, but at this time she was pale and wan. Fear was in her eyes. She clutched her breast and breathed shallowly, as if afraid the pain would worsen. The symptoms added up: her heart was failing her.

I knelt beside her and took her hand in mine. It was clammy. I felt for the heartbeat and found it erratic.

"Has she had such attacks before?" I asked.

The daughter answered, "She has complained of being very tired, but never has she been like this."

With great effort the woman raised her hand and spoke hesitatingly, "Twice . . . before . . . when the . . . family was away." Her breathing became yet more shallow. Her eyes were rolling back into her head. I was certain she was dying, and there was nothing I could do.

Paul had been watching. I felt his hand on my shoulder as he pushed me aside and knelt in my place. He placed his hand upon her forehead, lifted his eyes heavenward, and began to pray.

"Almighty God, I beseech you in the name of our Lord Jesus Christ for the sake of this woman, send your healing Spirit upon her. May she arise from this bed of affliction as a testimony of your love and power. May she be able to praise your name that she can take her place in her home with her family."

All was quiet in the room, but a strange feeling moved among us as if there were an unseen presence there. I have never gotten used to seeing the miracle of healing take place at any time. But to see it occur in this miraculous way was even more awe-inspiring. Color began to return to the woman's cheeks. Fear left her eyes. Strength flowed into her body.

Paul extended his hand to her. "Woman, arise!" His voice carried the tone of unequivocal authority. "The Lord has healed you. Praise his name!"

She stood on her feet, her face alive with wonder. Then she rushed to her husband's side, and he enfolded her in his arms. Her children flocked about her.

Tychicus raised his face toward the heavens and proclaimed, as tears coursed down his face, "Praise be to God for that which he has done this day. My beloved is restored to my bosom and to her children. Praised be the name of him whom he has sent, even Jesus Christ. I and my house shall forever worship him."

We remained in the home through the afternoon and returned to our abode before the evening of the next day.

The news of the healing spread throughout the city. Instead of being able to pursue our original plans to press on, we were detained by those who brought their sick and infirm for healing. Some brought cloths for Paul to touch that they might take them back to the ones they could not bring. But Paul also used the time to tell the gospel to all who would listen. Our stay extended into two months.

It was then that I saw the Lord use the "hedge of thorns" to send us on to do his will. It had been our intent to go into Bithynia, but such was not to be. God had other plans for Paul.

Chapter 9

One morning Paul took me aside. "Come, I have something to say to you." He led me to a place outside the city, and we sat beneath a tree. From here we could see people walking to and fro at the city gates. It was an ordinary day, but what Paul told me was to make it extraordinary.

"Luke," he said, drawing with a stick on the ground as he talked. "You know it has been my intent to go into Asia with the gospel." He paused as I nodded. "Something has happened to make me believe that the Lord has other plans for us."

I started to reply, but he stayed me with a gesture.

"Hear me out," he said. "I have not slept much for the past three nights. I have been visited by angels. Three stood at my bedside and looked upon me. My bosom was filled with apprehension. Then one extended his hand to touch my forehead, and my fear left. I was ready for whatever was to be required of me.

"The first two visits did nothing but fill me with a sense of power. Nothing was said, but I felt stronger than I have in a long time. I felt as if I could go forth and never be tired again. but the third visit crowned the whole. As the angels stood before me and pointed to the west, a voice came with resonance that shook my frame: 'Paul, thou art chosen of God for a great work. Send Silas to Timothy and bid him meet you in Troas. Leave this city and go to Troas, and it will be revealed unto you the will of the Lord.'

"At this moment Silas is getting ready to go to Lystra and bring Timothy to Troas with him. He will pass through Antioch. Perhaps you would like to send Porphia a message."

Paul was to go for Timothy! A flush of anger swept

through me. I blurted, "Why not send me? Then I could see my beloved wife."

Paul drew near me. I shrugged him off. Resentment was boiling up within me.

"Luke, my friend, I could have sent you, it is true. But this is an errand of urgency. Silas is young and strong. He will be able to travel faster. Besides, the trip to Troas is not easy. I need you with me as we journey lest I, in my foolish haste, fall prey to my old illness."

I knew his reasoning was sound. I had not even thought of returning to Antioch at this time until it seemed a possibility. Suddenly the longing for Porphia's arms about me became overwhelming. It was almost more than I could bear.

"I'll go and write a letter to Porphia," I said, disappointment still surfacing in my voice. "Thank you for that opportunity at least."

"Oh Luke, do not be angry with me," Paul pleaded. "We are called to the work of our Lord. We must do what is best."

"What *you* think is best," I replied with emphasis on the second word.

"That is unfair!" he exclaimed. "I have not made this decision without much prayer. You are right, it is my decision—but not without guidance."

We returned to the city, where I bought a piece of parchment on which to scribe a letter.

To my beloved Porphia. Every day is as a thousand when I am apart from you. I long to be beside you and to hold you close to me. I hope our journey will not last too long, for I want to return home to you and our son.

Much has befallen us since we parted. We were caught in a flood, but the Lord was with us and we were spared. Only one in the caravan was lost.

I have seen the healing power of God at work among the people of this city. One woman was dying and now lives because Paul was there. I have seen the sick healed, the lame walk, and the infirm strengthened.

Now we go to Troas. Our plans to go into Bithynia have been changed by angels of the Lord. Please find a scribe and write me to tell me how you and Lucian are faring. Silas will be returning to me and will bring me tidings.

The love I have for you grows stronger every day. May God bless and watch over you and bring us together soon.

I signed it with our own special symbol—a little drawing that meant much to us. It consisted of two parallel lines crossed toward each end with vertical lines to represent our closeness to one another. These were enclosed in a circle to represent the never-ending love of God who blessed our union.

Silas departed within the hour, and Paul and I began immediately to prepare for our journey to Troas. Instead of traveling from Mysia to Nicea of Bithynia, we were going to head almost straight west until we came into the mountains. There we would come to the highway which was the route from Adalia. The road was good, but there were places where it narrowed to only a few feet. Travelers were allowed to pass through these narrows by guards stationed at each end. But it was less dangerous than to try to scale the mountains through other passes.

Two days later, we set forth on our journey. By nightfall we had arrived at our first stop. Early the next morning we began the steep climb along the Roman road, and by nightfall we had almost reached the divide. These mountains were not as rugged as the ones we encountered en route to Mysia. Evergreens clothed them to their tops. The stones were flat, and the ground—when any could be seen—was dark and loamy. But it was the trees standing so majestically above us that made it seem we were walking through a gigantic temple of God.

By the evening of the third day I observed that Paul was less talkative than usual. He perspired profusely. Though he forced himself to keep up, his footsteps began to falter.

That night I made him let me check him. It became apparent that he was suffering another attack of ague. I knew then that he had been wise in insisting that I accompany him on this leg of our journey.

Through the night I poured liquids down his throat, with herbs to help allay his fever. By morning his fever was gone, but he was too weak to continue. We remained at the little inn while he rested. Though he fretted over the delay, I reminded him that this was better than for him to continue as he had when I first met him. Here we were safe and comfortable. If his fever stayed away throughout this day, we might be able to continue in the morning.

During the night I was awakened. Paul had turned over and was gently shaking me. "Luke, pray for me," he asked. "Pray that God will heal me so we may continue."

I was surprised that Paul would ask me to pray for him. I had seen the power of his prayers, but never had I been asked such a favor. What was I to say? What if God chose not to answer me?

Paul saw my hesitancy. "Do it!" he commanded.

I arose. Closing my eyes, I prayed within myself, "Oh God, Paul expects something to happen when I pray. You know that I have only the learning of the physician, and that is limited as compared to what you can do. For his sake, please answer my petition."

Going to Paul I laid my hands on his head and prayed. Never before had I prayed with such fervency. As I did so assurance came that what I asked was pleasing to God. All doubt left me, and when I had ceased and stepped back, I was confident that Paul would be all right.

"Thank you," he said quietly, and with that he lay back and went to sleep.

Strangely enough, when I lay back down it was in peace. My mind was at ease. I, too, slept.

When morning broke I was wide awake. Paul was not in his bed. I hastened to arise, calling his name.

"I am here," I heard him say. Hastening to the courtyard, I found him gathering our belongings together. "It is about time you awoke," he said. "Get the rest of our things together. We will join the group leaving today."

I looked at Paul with wonder. There was no sign that he had been ill. His hand was steady. His vision was clear. He moved with his usual alacrity. The Lord had blessed us both: Paul with health, me with a stronger faith.

By evening we had arrived at Adramyttium, a mercantile town with important relations in both the East and the West. We decided not to press on, for we were told that there were several streams to ford on our way to Troas. So we did not start until the next day.

Our pathway led us along the shore of the gulf. We would descend to the pebbly beaches, then climb over the rocks. Streams flowed from the many-fountained cliffs of Ida. It was late afternoon when we arrived at Troas located near where the famous city of Troy had once flourished. Nine successive cities had been built and had fallen during several thousand years. The Romans called the area Illium, but nothing of its former greatness remained. This city that once was the gateway to the rich wheatlands of Asia now was just a small community of people struggling to make a living. Ships put into port, picked up cargo, and sailed on. It was but another short stop along their way.

Equanius, a man I had known in Antioch, now a dealer in grain, was our host. He gave us a room with good ventilation. Night had hardly fallen before I was in bed, weary from the journey. Four days later we were joined by Silas and Timothy. They had journeyed fast and furiously, not wasting time. With them came a letter from Porphia.

To my beloved Luke I send all of my love. It was good to hear from you, and I thank God you are safe. Lucian and I are well. I would that you were here, but since you cannot be, I must share news with you. I guess our last night together was specially blessed, for the seed you have planted is growing and I am with child. I hope you can be home before I deliver. I miss you very much. May God bless you and bring you safely home.

Beneath her signature was our special sign, then the words: "Scribed by Amon."

As I read and reread her letter my heart leaped within me. We were soon to be blessed with another child. Oh, how I longed to be with her!

That very night I was awakened and found Paul sitting up in his bed. His eyes were wide open but he was not seeing things the normal eye can see. Every muscle in his body was taut. Then, as I watched, he was released and he lay back gently and closed his eyes. His face was serene. For a moment I was alarmed for fear that he had been stricken by some strange malady but as I watched, his breathing became normal. I touched his skin and it was without fever.

With my touch Paul awakened. He looked at me quizzically and I told him of what I had seen.

"Ah Luke, my friend," he said, his voice low and throbbing with emotion, "the message has come. This night I saw a man of Macedonia in this room. He called me by name and said, 'Paul, come to Macedonia. There are many souls that perish for want of the word of God.' The call has come."

He was calm, but his eyes held a light as they always did when he was looking for new fields to conquer. Now I knew where we were going. We would cross the sea to Macedonia.

Chapter 10

The next morning we walked to the harbor where we found a ship scheduled to sail to northern Macedonia within the hour. The captain said he would head for Neopolis at the mouth of the Gangites River. The wind was right, and the trip should take but two days. We collected our belongings and boarded the vessel.

As I stood near the bow, I could watch the prow cleave its way through the waters. We went through the strait between Tenedos and the mainland, then sailed past the Dardanelles and neared the eastern shore of Imbros. As we rounded the northern end of the island we could see in the distance the high ground of Samothrace, which had appeared to be a higher promontory of Imbros. The wind was two or three points abaft the beam as we shifted more to the west.

Although I had long worshiped the one God and now was a follower of his Son, Jesus Christ, the ancient traditions caused me to have strange feelings as we neared the shelter of the coast of Samothrace. I recalled the old superstition that Neptune's throne was on the peak of this island, high above all else. I thought of how his cave was believed to be beneath the waters of the sea nearby. It was then that I realized how hard the teachings of our youth die, and how easily what we once were can claim us from what we have become.

The sun was sinking toward the horizon, setting the sky and water afire, by the time we dropped anchor in the shelter of this place. No one went ashore for, though this was a safe anchorage, there was no good harbor anywhere on the island. It was a good stopping place, especially along the north shore when the wind came from the south.

During our daylong journey, Paul had not been idle. By the time we arrived at anchorage, a goodly number of the passengers and some of the crew had assembled about him as he told of the Christ.

"I am here to proclaim that the one true God is not afar off but is actively involved in our lives. Through his son, Jesus Christ, he has proclaimed a better way of life. All are of one blood, for God has so willed. All who seek him shall find him, for he is not far away. He teaches all to be just and true, and those who follow his ways need not fear, for he is their protector and comforter," Paul said. His listeners showed varying degrees of interest. Some crowded close to him and asked many questions. The message had a great effect on them. Several wanted to become followers, too. The Spirit of the Lord had moved in their midst even as we moved in the pathway into which the "wall of thorns" had thrust us.

The next morning, as the sun began to color the sky with its rays, crew members took their posts, hauled up the anchor, and set the sails to catch the south wind. We were not able to run before the wind, but it was strong enough that, in spite of the easterly current, we made good headway toward our destination.

It was midafternoon when we arrived at the port of Neapolis. Mountains rose high behind it, but the city was located on a promontory with a port on each side. We disembarked and, after pausing long enough to baptize the converts, Paul insisted that we make our way to the western edge of the city where we found an inn. The converts had taken up a collection among them and insisted that we use it to help us along our way.

That night Paul told of his plans. We sat before him and listened attentively.

"The nearest city to us that could serve as a missionary base is Philippi," Paul said, gesturing toward the mountains to the west. "The river that formed this delta flows past the city. Neopolis is a busy seaport, but it is not a place where we can settle down for a period of time and get the work of the church settled. Also, Philippi has the status of a colony. This makes it important to us, for the military roads lead to it, and it is there that garrisons of soldiers are stationed as a safeguard of the frontier. This city can be the hub of a wheel from which we can work with considerable safety to spread the gospel. You know that trouble seems to follow us. Our citizenship of Rome can stand us in good stead, for we will not be treated as strangers who are without the safeguard of Roman justice."

"I know a man in Philippi. His name is Clement," I offered. "His father and my father were at Alexandria at the same time. I have not seen him for several years, but I am certain that he will help us when we arrive."

"Good! Perhaps he can tell us where the Jews have their synagogue," Paul responded.

"I do not think there are many Jews in the city," I said.

"The Jews of the diaspora have settled everywhere." he assured me. "There will be some in a city of the importance of Philippi."

We agreed to follow the river road to Philippi the next morning. It was the day before the Sabbath, so we would need to leave early to cover the distance before the evening began.

By sunup we had gathered our belongings and were walking along the road that led to the canyon. We were not alone on the way. Ahead of us was a string of pack animals laden with goods that perhaps had come in on the very ship we had taken from Troas. A burly man kept the plodding animals moving. As we caught up with him he called, "Ah, fellow travelers! Are you headed for Philippi?"

Silas answered, "Yes. We hope to be there before evening."

Throw your bundles on that last animal and walk with me. The way is long, and I enjoy company."

"That is kind of you," said Timothy, unburdening himself.

"I am Luke, the physician," I offered as I, too, lay my load across the broad pack.

"I am Goram, the trader," our benefactor said. "I travel this road once each week."

"This is Silas, and that young man is Timothy," I said. "We came in from Troas yesterday." I turned, then, and continued, "Goram, meet my friend, Paul."

Each nodded, but when their eyes met, Goram bowed to him. "Are you the Paul who speaks of the resurrected God?" he asked. "I have heard of you in the marketplace."

"Yes, I am," replied Paul.

With that introduction, Paul took charge of the conversation. All through the day, even when we paused for refreshment at the riverside, he expounded on the message of Jesus Christ.

The sun was low in the sky by the time we arrived in Philippi. We parted from Goram after asking him if he knew of my friend Clement. He directed us to a shop near the center of the city. Paul told Goram of our intent to meet with the Jews, and he told us where they met.

There were few Jews, and the majority were women. At this time of the year they met at the riverside—as was the custom of Jews who had lived by the sea—to offer their prayers at the water's edge.

We made our way to Clement's shop. Just as we located it and were nearing its entrance, a disturbance began. Out of the door came two men. One had the other by the nape of the neck, propelling him with such violence that, when he shoved him toward the street, the man sprawled across the pavement. He quickly arose and hastened away. The taller man, standing in the doorway, shouted, "Stay out! You are lazy and useless to me. I could teach a child to do as much work as you do. Go! Go, go, go!" Following that outburst he turned to reenter the shop.

"Hold it," I cried, recognizing Clement. "Is this the way to greet an old friend?"

He turned and peered at me. As recognition flooded his face the frown was replaced with a smile.

"Luke! Is that really you?" He rushed to embrace me. "What are you doing here?"

With this, he escorted us inside, all the while asking questions faster than I could answer.

"One question at a time!" I cried.

We stood back and looked one another over. Then Clement spoke apologetically. "I'm sorry for the trouble at the door. I just got rid of one of my lazy employees. He was always dreaming instead of working and, when he worked—if you could call it working—he was so careless that often I had to do much of it over again." He turned and gestured toward a pile of tent cloth. "And I have an order that should be ready in twelve days."

He stood there, staring at the pile for a moment, then turned to us. "Enough of my problems," he proclaimed. "What brings you here?"

I introduced my companions. "Clement, meet my friend, Paul. And this is Silas. The young man by the door is Timothy. We have come to your fair city to tell of the wonderful things God has done for us."

"And where will you be staying?" Clement asked.

"I thought you might suggest some place," I replied. "It is almost the Sabbath, and we want to worship with the congregation of the Jews."

"I have but a humble dwelling at the rear of the shop, but you are welcome to spend the night with me," he offered.

"It is kind of you to offer," Paul interjected, "But we might be too many for such short notice."

"Not a problem," Clement replied. He clapped his hands, and a youth came running. "Go tell your mother that we have guests."

The youth scurried out of the room. Clement closed and barred the doors of the shop, then escorted us to his living quarters.

"I can't let you stay anywhere else. Maybe I'm selfish, but I am curious about this mission of yours. You must tell me about it."

His wife was shy, but she made us feel welcome. By the time we had washed the dust of travel away she had prepared a meal for us. It was simple but wholesome food, and we thoroughly enjoyed it after having had only ship's rations and the spicy food of the inn.

After the meal, we sat about the room and Paul began to speak of our reason for coming to Macedonia. As the story unfolded, the family sat spellbound. The experience of the flood impressed the children. The narration of the healings brought tears to the eyes of Clement's wife, who had lost her sister to a malady with symptoms similar to those Tychicus' wife had suffered.

"Oh that you had been here," she wailed. "My sister might be alive today."

Then Paul began to tell her of life after death. The glory of the resurrection brought her comfort, and she began to smile once more.

Pallets were spread on the floor for us, and after our

prayers we lay down to sleep. I was pleased with Paul's health. His strength was back, and his steps were light. Then I began to think of Porphia and wondered how she was feeling. I longed to fold her in my arms and to feel her sweet breath on my cheek as she snuggled close to me. I lay awake for a long time, but finally fell asleep.

Chapter 11

Early on the Sabbath we made our way to where the Jews were seated beside the quiet waters. Paul introduced us and was given a place beside the leader. When the time came for expounding, he was asked to speak. Without hesitation, he stood before them.

"The God of our father Abraham, Isaac, and Jacob has, in times past, blessed our people with guidance and has rescued us from danger. Who among us does not remember the words of the prophets that called us to task when we strayed from the way of righteousness?

"Our fathers did not always walk in the ways of God and broke the laws from time to time so that Jehovah brought upon them hard times and persecutions. They were driven out of the land of promise and, even today, are scattered to the farthest reaches of the earth.

"But God is a faithful God, and has promised that we would be a powerful people."

As Paul spoke, his listeners nodded in approval. Their expectations were rising, for he spoke as one about to reveal still greater things. He continued.

"Is there one of you who has not heard the words of the prophets who have promised that there would come one of the seed of David's house, who would drive out the conqueror and free his people from oppression?

"I come to proclaim that God has, in this time, sent into our midst the Anointed One. He walked among us and taught our people of his ways. He is Jesus of Nazareth.

"But our leaders were blind to what he taught. So bound to the traditions of those who have gone before that they could not identify the truth of God, they sought him out and slew him."

A gasp went through the gathering. It had never occurred to them that the leaders could err.

"I too once persecuted this Jesus, but he sought me out and saved me from the error of my ways. I am here to proclaim that he has brought to us the way of life once taught through the prophets. He has taught of the love of God for all creation. Every one is dear to him. Through him the Spirit of God is exercised and the sick are healed, the lame walk, and the blind are made to see."

A flurry of excitement swept through the congregation. One woman stood out from the others. Her mien was gentle, and goodness revealed itself as she moved and spoke. Now she focused her full attention on Paul. She was moved even more when he spoke of the resurrection and of the life to come. When he sat down, she was the first to his side. She introduced herself as Lydia. Then she invited us to her home, and we accepted.

We learned that Lydia was from Thyatira, a city across the sea. In her home town she had learned about dyes, and following her husband's death she had continued his business of dealing in dyes. She had prospered well in Philippi. Her seven children were a blessing to her, and her two oldest sons helped in the business.

That night the whole family assembled, and Paul again shared his message. One after another nodded in agreement. They were reluctant for us to retire, but the day had been eventful and we were tired.

Lydia invited her friends to come to her home to hear the words of Paul. Difficult questions were asked, and many heated discussions followed. But the Spirit of God prevailed, and many came to believe. Lydia was the first to speak publicly about it. Her whole household followed. It made a beautiful picture when they were escorted, one at a time, into the waters of baptism.

Others followed, and a congregation was organized.

During the days that followed Paul worked in Clement's shop to help him meet the deadline on his orders. This provided both income and the opportunity to talk to many people. Few who came in contact with Paul went away without knowing something about Jesus.

"It seems as if the Lord leads them to me," he said on one occasion. "And when they come, the opportunity always arises for us to talk of important matters. This opens the way for each to learn of the truth in Jesus."

"Yes, and I am kept busy with those who come to Lydia's," I added. "It seems as if there are not enough hours in the day to get all cared for. My name as a physician brings many, and it always seems to lead to a discussion of the power of God in our lives."

"That is the way it is," Paul mused. "Silas and Timothy are meeting people on the street, and many of those show up at our nightly meetings. In fact, as soon as I get this work caught up for Clement, I plan to join them."

A week later Paul was in the streets of Philippi daily, proclaiming the way of the Lord. His emphasis was on the kingdom of God and the expected return of Jesus Christ. This was exciting news to many, and they followed him to listen whenever they could.

A young woman who started following Paul and Silas wherever they preached was owned by some men who used her for their gain. She had an affliction which would come upon her whenever she was under stress. She would enter into a catatonic condition, during which she would become rigid and her jaws would lock. When she came out of the state, she would babble meaningless phrases. Her owners had taught her, under the inducement of pain and reward, to proclaim words from the ancient mystics. So clever were they at this that she had gained quite a reputation as a soothsayer and had made a handsome living for her masters. However, she posed a problem to the disciples. In the midst of their preaching, she would have a seizure and come out of it proclaiming, "These men are the servants of the most high God, which show unto us the way of salvation."

The interruptions were becoming more numerous, and each time she reaped a shower of coins from those nearby, for this had been the custom among them.

Though there was nothing the young woman said that could be faulted, her profession made it appear that Paul and Silas were identified with her in her soothsaying. This clouded the true miracles and gifts that accompanied their preaching. Nightly, Paul prayed for guidance in how to deal with the matter.

One morning the young woman appeared again. Paul fixed his eyes on her, and she drew near to him and knelt. Perceiving the kind of spirit that had possessed her, he said in a loud voice, "I command you in the name of Jesus Christ to come out of her."

Immediately a change came over her, and she appeared normal. The affliction had left her. Her owners did not realize what had happened until they sought to use her for their purposes again, but she could not do their bidding. She had no more seizures and her ability to babble the quotations was lost. It was a financial disaster to them, and they went to the rulers of the city to complain. Paul and Silas were arrested and hauled to court.

"These men are Jews and are causing trouble in our city," they accused, using ancient prejudices to aid their cause. Few of the Jews were Roman citizens and, therefore, were deprived of certain advantages.

The rulers, allowing their own prejudices to take over, miscalculated. Paul and Silas were scourged and questioned, but not allowed to plead their case. When directed to confess their guilt, they would not do so. Then they were thrown into jail and bound in fetters.

When word of this reached Lydia she immediately went to the magistrates to demand a release. Her pleading was to no avail. Instead, they scolded her for associating with malcontents and had her forcibly ejected from their presence. It was not until the next day that we learned of their plight and all that had happened to them while they were in prison.

Neither Paul nor Silas was disheartened. Though they had been beaten, they felt that their stripes were for the cause of Jesus. They had prayed and sung hymns through the night. As they did, their voices had carried throughout the building and had caused the other prisoners to take heart.

Toward the middle of the night there had come a rumbling as if an earthquake were taking place. As it grew louder, the walls and floors heaved. The prison doors were opened, and the fetters of the prisoners fell from them. The stocks in which their feet had been placed broke apart. The prisoners were free, but none moved from their places.

The jailer was frightened by the cataclysm, but now that he had survived it, he faced a greater danger. With the doors of the prison open, he was certain that all of his prisoners would escape. He also knew that the jailor would have to serve out the sentence of each escapee. Cold despair clutched his heart. He drew his sword and was about the fall on it when he heard a voice from the innermost part of the prison.

"Do yourself no harm; for we are all here." It was Paul speaking.

The jailer called for a torch and quickly made the rounds. Every prisoner was in his place. All could have left, but none did.

Suddenly there flooded through his mind all the stories he had heard about these two men. He remembered miracle after miracle. On one occasion he even had heard Silas preach and had thought he made more sense than most of the itinerate speakers. Now there had been a miracle for him. The power from their God had opened the jail for them, but they had not forsaken him in his time of peril. The love and mercy of the Savior whom they preached lighted his soul, and this man—who had imprisoned many—found himself in the bonds of love. He threw himself at the feet of Paul and Silas and cried, "What must I do to be saved?"

Paul reached down, and lifted him up. "Believe on the Lord Jesus Christ, and you and your household will be saved," he said simply.

The jailer took them to his rooms and applied salve to their wounds. Members of his family had gathered around to look with awe on these men whom the Lord had released. Paul shared the message of Jesus simply and fervently. That very night another household was added to the fold.

The next morning Lydia and I were at the doors of the rulers of the city. They would not see us. We were joined by others, and finally—in exasperation—they sent a lictor to the prison with instructions that the prisoners be freed and escorted to the gates of the city with instructions not to return.

To our delight, word came back from the prison. "These men refuse to be released," the lictor proclaimed. "They say they are Roman citizens, and that you have beaten them and imprisoned them without trial. They say that they will not leave until you, the magistrates who imprisoned them by decree, come to the prison and apologize and release them by your own hands."

Consternation blanketed them. The error of judgment came home with a hard fact: if an appeal was made to Caesar, not only might they lose their exalted positions but the whole city might lose its favored designation as a colony. With fear and dread, they made their way to the jail. There they found the prisoners in their places, manacled and in stocks. With profuse apology, they approached the men. With their own hands, they unfastened the bolts to release them, then personally escorted them outside. They pled, for the sake of peace, that these men leave the city.

But Paul was not to give them immediate satisfaction. His righteous indignation at having been treated unjustly was not fully appeased by their apology, because they had tempered it with the watered-down plea for him to leave. He was firmly determined that the work be left with strong leadership, for this city was to him an important base of operation. Several days passed before he began to make preparations to leave.

Paul's delay infuriated his enemies. They went through the city gossiping among the idlers in the streets and stirring up considerable opposition to Paul. They were afriad to act openly against him because the rulers of the city were wary of anything they might say. So it was that they secretly sought to kill him.

When word of the attempt was brought to Paul, he decided to leave the city for the sake of the congregation. He asked Timothy and me to remain behind to strengthen the work. From among those he had baptized, he set apart elders to take charge of the work. Lydia was made a deaconess and charged to see that the needy were cared for. She took a special interest in the young woman Paul had healed, and whose faith had become an inspiration to the congregation.

We saw Paul and Silas off to Thessalonica, the largest city in Macedonia and one of considerable importance. It was a free city, so it enjoyed self-rule and was not required to garrison soldiers, as was a colony. The weather was cold for winter was upon us. Rather than take the high road along the higher elevations, Paul chose to follow the road that paralleled the seashore. He and Silas would stop in Amphipolis, then Apallonia. It was their intent to take three days for the journey. The choice was partially due to my advice, for I wanted Paul to conserve his strength. Though he showed great improvement for one who had suffered debilitating illnesses I felt it would be best for him to go slowly, rather than press on as if Thessalonica would not be there if they delayed. So it was that we bade them farewell.

Chapter 12

The work in Philippi flourished. The persecution by the former owners of Tanka, the young woman healed of the false spirits, ceased with the exodus of Paul and Silas. They had thrown her out after her healing. That was when Lydia took her into her home. Goram, the trader, found her attractive and they were often together.

One day Goram came to me and asked if we might talk. We retired to the garden and sat beneath a tree Then I turned to him questioningly.

"It is about Tanka," he started, then fumbled for words.

"You find her desirable," I stated. There was no question in my mind.

"Yes," he replied hesitatingly, then went on. "I find her to be the sweetest person I have even known, but . . . " here he hesitated again.

I thought I could perceive what was troubling him.

"You wonder about her former affliction and whether or not it will come back?" I asked.

"Yes, I guess that is it. What caused her to be that way?" he asked.

"There are demonic forces at work in people's lives all about us. They may suddenly take over in persons and change them so much you would hardly know them. Sometimes they creep in slowly and the change is so gradual it is hardly noticeable. Occasionally they appear to have taken over at birth, through some fault of the parents. But there is one thing I have noted: they are never satisfied until the takeover is complete and they have total control over their victims," I explained.

"I have seen that in a few," Goram stated, "but I have never met one who was cured."

"There is no question in my mind that Tanka is healed and that the affilliction will not return," I affirmed.

"Do you think her owners will try to take her back?"

"I do not think so. Not only is she of no use to them now but their masquerade has been exposed. They cannot use some other unfortunate person in the same manner because their credibility has been shattered."

"Is that why they have been so angry?" Goram asked.

"Perhaps," I replied. I thought for a while, then went on. "I believe Tanka has been blessed with more than just being cured of her affliction and freed from her unjust masters."

"How do you come to that conclusion?" he asked.

"Well, not only have those blessings been given her, but she has been given a greater freedom. She now is free to choose. One of the great choices she has made is to be a follower of Jesus Christ."

"That is true," he agreed.

"And something else," I added. "Should you ask her, she is free to choose to love you."

Goram's face lighted up. He sat there for a few moments longer; then he arose and rushed out of the garden. In my mind I imagined that he was going to seek Tanka. Three days later my surmise was verified. Goram and Tanka came to me to declare their love for one another.

Tanka, blushing beautifully, and Goram, standing proudly, were the picture of two people in love. I could not help feeling a twinge in my breast; Porphia and I shared such a love and I longed to have her by my side.

"I have spoken to Lydia," Goram began, "and she has

assured me that we have her blessing. I have gone before the magistrate, and he has assured me that she is free to wed. He even prepared this paper." He handed a piece of parchment to me.

"For all to know: The slave, Tanka, having been abandoned by her masters and having proven that she is able to care for herself and not be a burden on the government, is hereby decreed to be a free person in charge of her own destiny." The paper was signed by the magistrate and sealed with his own seal as an agent of Caesar.

"I am surprised that you were able to get such a paper," I exclaimed.

"I think they were still smarting from their experience with Paul and decided that this might appease us," Goram offered. "Besides, I am not without influence here because I bring a goodly amount of trade to the city."

"You may be right," I conceded.

Two days later the two were wed. Lydia gave Tanka a beautiful ornamented gown with slippers to match. They went up into the mountains to be alone for a while, and when they returned they took their place in the congregation.

Timothy was a good missionary. Though some looked askance at his youthfulness, when he spoke they soon realized he had wisdom beyond his years. Nearly every day he would bring inquirers to our meetings. Often we would spend most of the night in discussions. People hungered for the meat of the gospel. We fed them daily and, to our store of knowledge, more was added through prayers and devotions.

It was drawing close to spring, and we had not heard from Paul or Silas. Some questions about the Resurrection had been raised, and we were unable to find answers that satisfied us. We armed Timothy with an epistle of inquiry and sent him to find Paul. He was anxious to see his spiritual father who, on the occasion of his circumcision, had said, "This day have I begotten you."

Without Timothy to assist, I was kept so busy that I had little time to practice my profession. A stranger from Sardica, a city high in the mountains west of Philippi, contacted us through Goram. He remained to hear more of the message, and after six days he begged us to send someone back with him to his home. Goram agreed to go, leaving Tanka with Lydia until his return.

At last we received an epistle from Jerusalem. It had been dictated many months before and had been carried first to Lystra, then to Antioch, and finally to us. It contained word of their need for a conference with those in the field in order that they might discuss some of the problems that had arisen. After we had made a copy for ourselves, we dispatched one of our young men to carry the message to Thessalonica. Within it were many words of counsel and the testimony of Andrew.

From Egypt Andrew reported the growth of the church there. He had run into a number of Jews who readily accepted the message but wanted to make it a part of a larger volume of teachings from the East. The result of this odd mixture of religious thoughts was a confusing doctrine. Taking the trend for polytheism of the Eastern beliefs, they modified the teachings of Jesus regarding the Father, Son, and Spirit. Adding to it theories regarding angels and demons, they introduced a teaching that salvation is dependent on knowing all of the truth. God, the father, was all-knowing because he knew more than any of those who lived in the universe. A descending scale of knowledge placed Jesus, the Holy Spirit, and angels on increasingly lower planes of knowledge until they passed from the spiritual world into the material world. Human beings were at the dividing line, while demons were farther down the scale. From the ideas of reincarnation, they taught that individuals could move from the material world through gaining knowledge. Such knowledge involved knowing what to eat and drink, how to conduct one's self, understanding the mysteries of the universe, and a myriad of other areas to which more were added daily.

In his letter Andrew warned us against the heresy; to it were added the signatures of Peter and James. "Be careful of the man who says, 'I know,' and then proceeds to exalt himself and degrade others," Andrew wrote.

We felt that such teachings were far from us but took note of how easy it was to stray from the truth. We anxiously awaited word from Paul regarding our own questions.

With the epistle from Andrew came a message from Porphia. I read it with great joy.

My beloved Luke, from his loving wife, Porphia: I long for you always and wish you were here to see how Lucian is growing. Your letter from Troas was most welcome. I carry it next to my bosom and read it often. Yes, my love, I have learned to read. Note that I am writing this with my own hand, though I have some help from Marconius. I am proud of you as you care for our dear friend Paul, but even more proud that you are able to help spread this gospel. The work here is growing as numbers are added to our congregation almost every week. I hope you can come to me before long, for I miss you greatly.

Once again the pangs of homesickness gripped my soul. I knew it would be many more months before I could see my beloved wife again. The demands of the work were great, though some of the elders were now able to carry more of the responsibilities than before.

Nearly two months after he had left, Timothy returned bearing word of the events in Thessalonica.

When Paul and Silas first arrived in the city, a tour of the area revealed much wickedness. There was a station where sailors came after many weeks at sea. They fell prey to various religious cults in which fertility rites were considered to be the essence of life. The phallic symbol was to be seen everywhere. Day and night extravagant orgies took place, many in public, where sexual excesses were practiced.

Paul struck hard at this when he began his work at the synagogue. He was an immediate success. Encouraged by this he stayed on, taking residence at the home of Jason. Here he used his trade as a means of support.

In his message he emphasized the kingdom of God and the second advent of Christ. So fervent was his teaching, that it touched the Thessalonians deeply—but they did not fully understand the message. What they did get led them to believe that the second coming of Jesus Christ was imminent. Life was short, and judgment was nigh. They looked about them and realized how vain the ways of the world were. The result was that they saw no reason to plan for tomorrow. They quit working, lived on their assets, and sat about discussing the teachings in lofty ways. Those who had much cared for those who had little, as they looked forward to the day of the coming of the Lord.

Out of this grew opposition. The Jews saw that they were losing influence. The synagogue congregation had already been heavy with Gentiles, and now it was more so. They began talking to the people in the marketplace, telling them Paul was teaching that all should become idlers. They intoned their concern that soon all commerce would stop. They also whispered that there was a subversive element in this new teaching, for it spoke of the overthrow of Rome and the rule of Jesus Christ.

Their whispering campaign was fruitful. Mobbers gathered and advanced on the house of Jason. They shouted. They stoned the building and demanded that Paul and Silas be turned over to them. When they were not to be found, they took Jason and his family before the rulers. Their accusation was that they disrupted the commerce of the city and proclaimed Jesus as successor to Caesar.

The rulers recognized the seriousness of the charge. After much questioning, they found that there was no threat in the teachings but knew this would not satisfy the mob. They were able to meet the dilemma with a clever strategy, however. They placed Jason under a peace bond. Now the problem rested on him. He had to maintain peace.

This put Paul in an untenable position. If he remained, the threat of another riot was always there. Finally he decided to go to Berea, a journey of about one day.

At the time of their departure to Berea Timothy was sent back to Philippi with instructions to see if the work was strong enough for me to leave and join him. Timothy was to return, also.

Chapter 13

I assessed the situation carefully and, after meeting with the elders, decided to join Paul. Timothy would remain in order to finish some of the work we had begun.

One of the new projects grew out of Goram's return from Sardica. He reported that he had baptized the members of three households and a number of others. He asked that he and Tanka be allowed to return to strengthen the work. It was agreed, but Timothy felt that he needed to spend some time teaching Goram the things he had learned.

So it was that I departed Philippi. I stopped for a day in Thessalonica to visit the members then proceeded to Berea. On my arrival, I found Paul jubilant with success. The Jews had been very hospitable and had diligently searched the scriptures to verify his teachings. They could find no fault with what he taught. The message was accepted by many, some of whom were the wives of the most honorable men of that community.

We labored until the beginning of summer. At that time word had gotten back to Thessalonica of Paul's whereabouts. Seething with anger, the ones who had caused him trouble there were sent to Berea. It was apparent that their anger was directed toward him—not toward the believers—so we knew he must go to another place. We found a ship headed for Athens. Sopater, Paul, and I embarked, leaving Silas behind, assured that Timothy would soon join him.

Paul was deeply disturbed over the way the Jews had dogged his footsteps all the way from Thessalonica. His great desire was to preach the message to them, but all he got for his efforts was persecution.

When I reminded him that many Jews had accepted the gospel, he exclaimed gloomily, "But not enough!"

We left Berea at the base of Olympus. The broad plain extending to the seashore began to fall away as we sailed from the port of Dium. Olympus, with its dark woods seeming to wrap it in a cloak of mystery, was capped with snow. Here, many believed, was where the gods dwelt. With the dropping away of the shore, Paul's mood began to change.

"Luke," he said as he lay on his pallet at the side of the ship, "it may well be that this is God's way of letting me introduce the gospel more fully."

Leaving my own thoughts behind, I asked, "What do you mean?" I wondered if he had received another vision.

"Athens is noted for its philosophers. It is apparent that they are religiously inclined for they worship gods of every kind and nature." He spoke slowly and deliberately as he sought to put his thoughts into words that would be meaningful to me.

"They have great influence over the thinking of the Greeks," he continued. "If I am able to show them the better way through Jesus Christ, they can carry the message throughout the world. Through them I have a ready-made missionary force."

His eyes glistened as he talked. Was it the reflection of the setting sun, or was it a holy light? I pondered his reasoning as I watched the shepherds on the hills above Tempe. They grew smaller and smaller with our progress over the waters

"I don't know, my friend," I replied. "It has been my observation that the philosopher likes to talk a lot but is short on doing."

We grew silent, each deep in thought. I was thinking of Porphia and wondering when I could see her again.

With the coming of night we huddled together with our cloaks around us for warmth. Besides the groaning of the ship and the flap of the sails occasionally we would hear a loud pop as we headed into another tack and the wind whipped the cloth into shape. Our last view before darkness was of the heights of Macedonia appearing as a floating island on the distant horizon. Then we slept.

During the night there had been a thudding of bare feet as the sailors went about furling the sails. Slowly we came to a halt. The anchor was cast, and we lay at rest awaiting the dawn. We would not try the harbor until it was light enough to avoid collision. I stirred from my slumber, looked about, and saw Paul sleeping soundly. I turned over and slept again.

When I awakened Paul was kneeling in prayer. I peered across the water. Piraeus, the harbor to the city of Athens, was visible in the distance. Farther on was Mount Morea. Clouds rested heavily upon the heights but the crown of the plain, the Acropolis, rose above them.

This was no small port. Many ships lay in the basin. But the past majesty of Athens was history. Though still a city of consequence, all was in a state of decay. The proud spirit of Greece had dissipated with the fall to Roman forces. However, through its teachers, Rome was beginning to be conquered by Greek thought. The military genius of Rome could not be doubted, but the Greek scholars who traveled throughout the empire were teaching Rome's children. Here, in my way of thinking, was where the real battle was being fought. The materialism of Rome had been pitted against the Greek love of beauty. A new ethic was certain to come forth.

It was midmorning before we arrived in the city of

Athens. Everywhere we went the religious bent of Greece was evident. There were statues dedicated to Apollo, the patron of the city, and little worship centers on nearly every ledge of rock: shrines of Venus, Ceres, Unwinged Victory, and Bacchus. Even the public buildings bore religious names: temple of the Mother of Gods, to Bacchus and Jupiter. Paul said little, but I knew his fertile mind was working. Suddenly we came upon a lone shrine. The inscription read, "To the Unknown God."

Paul stopped there a long time. It seemed as if he was transfixed and unable to move. At last he shook himself, pointed to the shrine and exclaimed, "That is it! That is it! They hunger for the God we know and they suspect."

I was not sure what he meant, but I stood there in wonder at the excitement that suffused his whole being.

Then he fell silent. We walked along the street until we came to the hill where the statue was raised to Aries. The Romans had named it Mars Hill after their counterpart of the Greek war god. I did not interrupt his musing, for I sensed he was deep in thought.

While we stood there on that hill, Paul said, "I think I know how to get their attention now."

We learned that the philosophers gathered on this hill to proclaim and debate their ideas. Every kind of religion, political concept, and moral issue was represented here. Each was accorded a chance to proclaim his ideas. There was a tacit agreement that all had a right to their opinons, but on occasion the enthusiasm of speaker and listener led to near riots. The hill was aptly named after the god of war.

We sought out the synagogue, where Paul once again proclaimed his views. There was great dispute among the Jews and the believers. Paul turned to the marketplace and found ready ears.

Among those who heard him were some Epicureans and Stoics. They banded together and invited Paul to speak at Mars Hill. What a combination—Stoics and Epicureans!

The founder of the Stoic school was Zeno, a native of Cyprus. He saw the degradation of the time and sought to combat it by forming his followers into a school of philosophers. Though they condemned the worship of images and the building of temples, they justified the belief in many gods as superior to none at all. To them, God was the spirit or reason of the universe. God did not create but merely reorganized that which already existed. They set for themselves a goal of austere self-denial. Their ideal was to be apathetic and untouched by human passion, to be unmoved by any change in the world about them. Reason was their byword; pride was their mien.

The Epicureans were atheistic. Materialism was their only reality. Though they did profess a kind of belief in gods, these were viewed as phantoms of reality and unable to exercise influence on the world. Since there was no creator, there was no moral government. As a result, the Epicurean's highest aim was self-gratification. The Epicurean goal was pleasure. The Stoic goal was pride.

There could have been no more unlikely banding together than the followers of these two philosophies who sought Paul out for debate. They struck at the heart of the matter when they put the question to him: "Tell us more of this Jesus Christ and the Resurrection. This is, indeed, a strange doctrine."

Paul was not bashful, even in the presence of great men. He had spoken before the chief magistrates of many cities. All were equal in his sight, for all were potentially God's children.

"Men of Athens," he began, "I have walked the streets

of your city. Everywhere I look I note that you are faithful to many gods. Indeed, I believe you are much too superstitious. I noted that you also have erected a shrine to an unknown god."

At his mention of the shrine, an electric shock ran through the group. Heads nodded in acknowledgment that they knew of which he spoke. Other faces revealed a smug complacency that seemed to imply that this was a touch of genius to so cover ignorance.

Paul continued, "Now that is the direction of superstition, for it causes you to worship that which you do not know. How can you give allegiance to that which you do not know, any more than you can come back from where you have never been?"

The smiles of complacency disappeared.

"I am here to save you from such folly," Paul went on. "I am here to proclaim that I know the name of that God. The God I proclaim created the heavens and the earth. He made them not with hands but by the power of his Spirit. It is he who created you and all people. It is he who set you in your place and others in theirs. In him we have our being. Without him we neither move or exist."

By now Paul had their undivided attention. This was strong medicine, and they did not want to miss any point of his argument. As Paul told them how God had sent Jesus Christ into the world and how he had raised him from the dead, a change came over the listeners. Up until now they thought of the resurrection as the name of a god. It had not occurred to them that it had to do with raising the Son of God from the grave.

A murmur of derision swelled among them, and the leaders began to turn away. "We must go now," they said, not meeting his eyes. "We will hear more from you later."

But Paul's sermon had stirred some. Damaris came with his friend Dionysius and invited us to his home. It was from this small beginning that the church in Athens got its start.

It never ceases to amaze me to note the manner in which the Spirit of God works as I think back over our journey. We left Antioch with a definite goal in mind. We had great plans to spread the work in Bithynia. We did not accomplish that goal, but went another way. Each place we visited, souls were brought into the church, but never were we allowed to settle down. When we thought all was going well, we found ourselves driven to another place. This could not be mere fate. There was intelligence behind it. Someone was always to catch the spark and nurture it to flame in their lives. Philippi—there was a city I could have settled in and been happy. I loved the people. It would have been good to have Porphia come to me there. But this did not happen. Paul called for me, and I went to him and ministered. But I did not feel at home in Athens. Though we made progress, I sensed that we would not be there long.

My apprehensions were justified one morning when Paul returned from his daily devotions on the promontory near the temple of the virgin. He found himself looking westward to the isthmus that was the land bridge to Corinth. As he stood there, he realized that Athens was not going to be the focal point of the work in Achaia. The people of this city, so provincial in nature, lived for the past. The gospel is for the present. Within Paul's breast swelled a familiar urge—he must be about the business of the Lord. This meant leaving behind those who could carry on in this place and moving out in a new direction. He voiced his decision to me, "We shall go to Corinth soon."

Biographical Sketch of
Alfred Harter Yale
September 28, 1913–February 21, 1984

Alfred Harter Yale was born to Samuel and Edith Yale on September 28, 1913, in Independence, Missouri. He had one sister, Mary Catherine Yale Gordon, who presently resides in Ft. Collins, Colorado. He died in Beaver, Pennsylvania, of cancer on February 21, 1984, at the age of seventy.

After graduation from William Chrisman High School in Independence, Missouri, he attended William Jewell College, receiving a B.A. in psychology. While attending this college he was also a student of the Bible. For six months he attended the Theology School of Southern Methodist University in Dallas, Texas, but did not graduate because his instructors could not answer, to his satisfaction, all of the questions he had about the doctrine that was being taught.

He was active in Scouting and, under the leadership of his father, Samuel Yale, worked for several years in Boy Scout troops. Both were members of the Order of Mic-O-Say in Kansas City. Alfred also served on the World Church Scout Committee for several years and was chaplain several summers at Bartle's Boy Scout Camp in Osceola, Missouri. He was the first Scout leader to take several of the boys on a fifty-mile hike from Independence to the Scout camp in Osceola, and back without any help. The *Independence Examiner* carried an article on this unusual hike. He received the Eagle Scout award and, with great pleasure and pride, was able to present the same award to his oldest grandson, Douglas Lewis.

Alfred married Tina Mae Cottingham on November 5, 1933; she died in 1941. One daughter was born to this marriage, Eleanor Marie Lewis, who gave him four grandchildren and two great-grandchildren. On October 4, 1942, he married Miriam Christine Winholtz who faithfully supported him in his ministry. He is survived by two daughters from this marriage: Nancy Louise Kwak, who gave him two granddaughters, and Maxine Miriam Bailey who gave him one grandson and one granddaughter. An unfortunate cloud came over this marriage and it was dissolved in February 1981. Miriam is currently living in Madison, Wisconsin, with her daughter, Nancy.

Alfred married Kay Marie Johnson (presently Mrs. Marlan Bryan) on August 19, 1983. He is survived by four stepchildren: Debra Tinker, William Burgess, Phillip Burgess, and Steven Johnson, as well as four stepgrandchildren.

Alfred was baptized into the Reorganized church August 8, 1948, in Salt Lake City, Utah, by Arthur Stoft; ordained a priest in January, 1949, and an elder the following September.

In 1950 he accepted church appointment and was ordained a seventy in 1952 and a high priest in 1958. He served as a missionary in Houston, Texas, and Topeka, Kansas. While in Des Moines, Iowa; Tulsa, Oklahoma; and Ogden, Utah, he served in pastoral positons. In Utah he was also an assistant to the district president and district solicitor. While in Des Moines he studied the Greek language at Drake University.

After moving to Independence in 1960 Alfred joined the staff at the School of the Restoration because of his knowledge of the scriptures. Later he became dean of the Extension Division and assistant to the First Presidency, serving in both of these capacities until

1974. After twenty-four years of giving much valued ministry, he retired from church appointment in 1974.

Alfred was the author of *Life and Letters of Paul*, coauthor of *Ordinances and Sacraments of the Church*, and editor of the *Priesthood Manual*.

Following his retirement he did counseling for five years in the Kansas City area.

He had many hobbies, including photography, woodcarving, leather work, painting, knitting, crocheting, needlepoint, music, and camping.

In 1980 he moved to the Toledo, Ohio, area where he directed the church choir and was a church soloist. He also served as a counselor to the pastor and as missionary coordinator.

The ministry Alfred Yale gave will long be remembered by those who knew and loved him.